Law, Ethics, and the War on Terror

Matthew Evangelista

polity

First published in 2008 by Polity Press

Polity Press
65 Bridge Street
Cambridge CB2 1UR, UK

Polity Press
350 Main Street
Malden, MA 02148, USA

ISBN-13: 978-0-7456-4108-9
ISBN-13: 978-0-7456-4109-6(pb)

A catalogue record for this book is available from the British Library.

Typeset in 10.25 on 13 pt FF Scala
by Servis Filmsetting Ltd, Stockport, Cheshire
Printed and bound in Great Britain by MPG Books Ltd, Bodmin, Cornwall

For further information on Polity, visit our website: www.polity.co.uk

Contents

List of Illustrations

Tables

Boxes

Preface

Most people intuitively feel that violating the Geneva Conventions or engaging in torture is wrong, yet they may not have a full grasp of the underlying legal details or an understanding of the ethical debates. The Global War on Terror has given these matters a certain urgency. The United States responded to the brutal attacks of 11 September 2001 by declaring itself at war. Its subsequent behavior, the capture and imprisonment of hundreds of accused 'enemy combatants', widespread evidence of torture and abuse of the detainees, and, finally, the invasion of Iraq have alarmed people at home and abroad.

Lawyers, philosophers, and ethicists have pursued these issues in their professional journals and to a certain degree in the public sphere. There are, however, few books that provide a basic overview for the non-specialist of the key ethical and legal issues in the war on terror. That is what the present book aspires to do. My own training is in history, literature, and political science rather than in philosophy or law. I have, however, been teaching in the area of international law and ethics since the mid-1990s, when I was on the faculty at the University of Michigan. In 1992 I had announced to my students that I would be exploring a new area of teaching, since I had become 'doubly obsolete' in my old ones. As a Sovietologist who studied and taught about the US–Soviet nuclear arms race, I had witnessed 'my' country and 'my' problem both disappear, thanks largely to the reforms of Mikhail

Gorbachev. He in turn had been inspired by a transnational network of disarmament activists, among whom Dr Randall Forsberg, the founder of the Nuclear Freeze movement, stood out for her energy, insight, and commitment. I dedicate this book to her memory.

Much of my teaching at Cornell, since I joined the faculty in 1996, has focused on ethical issues in international affairs. I had the privilege to co-teach a graduate seminar on that subject with Henry Shue, one of the most thoughtful scholars of international ethics. In the couple of years following the 9/11 attacks, I worked with my colleague, Professor David Wippman of Cornell Law School, to organize a conference and produce an edited book on the implications of the war on terror for the laws of war. I have learned a tremendous amount from David and the other participants in the project. I draw on some of the material from our book in this study, while accepting sole responsibility for any errors in my interpretation of the law.

Many of the ideas explored in these chapters first emerged as lectures, at Michigan and Cornell and at several institutions in Italy. In addition to thanking my US students, I would like to acknowledge students and colleagues at the Alta Scuola di Economia e Relazioni Internazionali (ASERI), Università Cattolica del Sacro Cuore, Milan; at the Dipartimento di Politica, Istituzioni, Storia, Università di Bologna, where I was a Visiting Fulbright Lecturer in 2006; at the Università Suor Orsola Benincasa in Naples; and at the International School on Disarmament and Research on Conflicts at Andalo (Trento). Thanks are due also to the organizers and participants of seminars where I presented early versions of some of these arguments: Brown University's Watson Institute; the Fondazione Mediterraneo in Naples; the Centro Einaudi in Turin; the Istituto per gli Studi di Politica Internazionale, Milan; Gamla Torget, Uppsala University, Sweden; the Tomsk State

University, Russia; and the Faculty of Law, Mohamed V University, Rabat, Morocco.

At Polity, I owe thanks to Louise Knight for proposing that I write this book; to her assistant, Emma Hutchinson; to the anonymous reviewers for their thoughtful comments; and to Manuela Tecusan, copy-editor and classicist, for, among other things, convincing me to replace *jus* with *ius*.

I am grateful to my wife, Joan Filler, and to my Cornell colleagues, Peter Katzenstein, Jonathan Kirshner, and Sidney Tarrow, for their helpful comments on the manuscript, and to a former colleague, Jeremy Rabkin, for discussions about some of the issues I cover here. The Peace Studies Program at Cornell has been a consistent source of support. I especially thank my longtime friend and colleague Judith Reppy and our irreplaceable staff, Elaine Scott and Sandra Kisner. I thank my mother for everything she did in raising me to stimulate my interest in ethical issues.

I wrote most of this book while visiting the home of my in-laws, Maurice and Myril Filler, stealing away time from the computer to enjoy lively discussions about the sorry state of our world. Their continued intellectual engagement, sense of optimism, and support for my work are a great source of inspiration.

Introduction

The mass murder of thousands of innocent civilians by al Qaeda terrorists plumbed the depths of criminality and immorality. The various responses to those attacks, particularly by the United States, provoked widespread accusations that the anti-terrorist cure may be worse than the terrorist disease. This book explores the key legal and ethical controversies that arose in the wake of the brutal acts of 11 September 2001 and of the launching of the Global War on Terror – a metaphorical and real war of indefinite duration and unlimited reach.

The Cold War ended with the fall of the Berlin Wall on 9 November 1989 – the *first* 9/11. The demise of communism in the face of peaceful mass protests, led by reform socialists and dissidents, capped a particularly productive decade of efforts to promote human rights worldwide. These efforts created the impression that a global civil society had emerged, to challenge the dominance of states and to establish new norms to guide their behavior, especially in the realm of human rights and limitations on warfare. The aftermath of the *second* 9/11, however, witnessed a reassertion of state prerogatives and a strengthening of executive authority in many countries. The US administration of George W. Bush alarmed many people, at home and abroad, by the policies it pursued in its war on terror – particularly its treatment of detainees at Guantánamo Bay and Abu Ghraib prisons, its defiance of the Geneva Conventions, its use of torture against terrorist suspects, and its invasion of Iraq. By the autumn of 2006, citizens polled in the United Kingdom, the closest US ally, viewed George Bush as a greater threat to world peace than either the North Korean leader, Kim Jong-Il, or the Iranian president, Mahmoud Ahmadinejad. Only Osama bin Laden came in ahead of Bush, at 87 percent to the US president's 75 percent. Other US allies and neighbors reported similar results.[1]

Whether or not the United States under George Bush constituted the greatest danger to international security, it certainly generated the most controversy. Yet the main issues that arose in the wake of the 9/11 attacks will long outlast the Bush administration. The purpose of this book is to provide the relevant historical and political background and the basic legal and ethical frameworks for some of the major controversies related to the war on terror. My goal is not to produce a law textbook or a philosophical treatise, but rather a general introduction, accessible to non-specialists. My overall theme is the tension between the efforts of two sets of actors. On one side are the proponents of enhancing human rights and increasing restrictions on warfare. These include nongovernmental organizations, some governments, and individuals – often characterized collectively as 'norm entrepreneurs'. On the other side are other governments, most notably the United States, pursuing the Global War on Terror, often at the expense of basic rights. I do not spend much time examining whether this terminology makes sense, whether one can wage a genuine war against a *thing*, such as terror, or the *tactics* of terrorism. Others have done so to good effect.[2]

My main argument is that the war on terror is bringing about a return to state prerogatives in establishing the norms that govern international behavior. This is, in fact, the predominant explanation for international law – that customary law comes primarily from state practice and treaty law reflects state interests. Yet, with the end of the Cold War, we seemed to experience something different: a greater influence on the part of civil-society groups and nongovernmental organizations.[3] That short period could well be ending now. Chapter 1 sets out the basic outlines of the argument about norms versus practice in the evolution of ethics and law. I use the chapter not to engage in a theoretical debate with legal scholars or political scientists, although some of their work informs my analysis.[4] Instead, I present the argument as a framework for evaluating the subsequent evidence from the controversies that have surfaced in the war on terror.

Chapter 2 addresses the first one of these: it is a controversy over the very definition of terrorism. The chapter examines whether government and military officials can be considered victims of terrorism, or whether the victims must be only innocent civilians. It explores the question of 'state terrorism' and the role of terror in warfare, particularly in aerial bombardment. It explains how the United Nations has sought to pursue conventions to cope with the threat of terrorism, all the while recognizing the unfortunate reality that often one state's terrorist is another's freedom fighter. It presents a possible compromise, which leads to a focus on terrorists who are non-state actors but which does not relieve states from their responsibilities when they commit war crimes and atrocities.

Chapter 3 tackles the main questions regarding the treatment of terrorist suspects: Do the Geneva Conventions apply? Who qualifies to be a prisoner of war and who decides on it? What are 'enemy combatants' and what are their rights, if any? The chapter discusses how the Bush administration and how the US Supreme Court have answered these questions. It then reviews the debate on torture, not only in its legal and ethical dimensions, but also by asking where the political initiative came from to subject detainees to harsh interrogations. Finally, the chapter considers the legality and practicality of targeted killings of suspected terrorists as a preventive measure.

Can someone suspected of planning a bomb attack be a legitimate target under the laws of war?

Chapter 4 is devoted to another preventive measure, equally controversial but more consequential: war. The chapter reviews the legal status of the wars in Afghanistan and Iraq, as well as their political motivations. It considers whether, despite the widespread global opposition to the Iraq War, states are coming to accept the idea of preventive measures against terrorism. Is a norm in favor of preventive war emerging?

Chapter 5 addresses a different category of wars – the ones fought for ostensibly humanitarian purposes. Both humanitarian interventions and wars for 'regime change' pose problems for aid organizations which strive to maintain neutrality and impartiality in the expectation that they will be accorded immunity from the violence. The situation during the early twenty-first century rendered those expectations increasingly unrealistic. The fate of aid workers is complicated by their interaction with the private security corporations upon which governments depend to carry out their humanitarian wars. The modern-day guns for hire rarely fit the technical legal definition of a mercenary, and thus fall into a kind of legal limbo. They seem unaccountable for the many crimes in which they have been implicated. This chapter, along with the preceding ones, reinforces the point that it is worth understanding the evolution of two types of norms: those that harm civilians and diminish human rights as well as those that protect civilians and expand their rights. A major factor influencing the evolution of the first kind of norms is the war on terror.

Readers will notice that most of the attention in this book is directed to the policies of the United States. It is not the only country engaged in a self-described war on terror. In a previous book I wrote about another one: Russia.[5] Others are writing systematically about a range of countries facing the 'international state of emergency' that 9/11 provoked.[6] In this book I occasionally mention examples from other states' experiences with terrorism. The United States, however, is the world's preeminent military power, with an annual war budget that exceeds the total military spending of the rest of the world.[7] The United States is also the principal target of the other main protagonist in the war on terror: the al Qaeda network of Islamist terrorists. This is not a book about al Qaeda, or even about terrorists per se. Except for the discussion of the debates over definitions in Chapter 2 and the status of enemy combatants and detainees in Chapter 3, I do not have a lot to say about terrorists. This is mainly a book about the evolution of norms and laws governing warfare and the protection of civilians during a war on terror. And here is the final justification for focusing on the United States: Most theories that accord state practice first place in shaping the evolution of norms would anticipate that the most powerful state in the system would be the most influential. I qualify this generalization at certain points in the book and in the concluding chapter, arguing that other states and nongovernmental organizations can still play an important role. This argument provides a small bit of hope in an otherwise bleak prognosis.

CHAPTER ONE

Norms versus Practice in International Law and Ethics

What we commonly call 'the laws of war' has two other names, used by professionals in the field: 'international humanitarian law' and 'the law of armed conflict'. Which name you use says a lot about how you think about the sources and purpose of law in the international system. Members of humanitarian organizations and many international lawyers prefer the name 'international humanitarian law'. They date the modern emergence of this body of law to the efforts of Swiss businessman Henry Dunant, founder of the International Committee of the Red Cross (ICRC). Dunant convened the first meeting of the ICRC in 1863. He was inspired by the horrors he witnessed at the Battle of Solferino in northern Italy four years earlier. The committee was initially formed to aid wounded soldiers; it then expanded its scope to include sailors, and later, prisoners of war. As war became increasingly destructive to civilians, the ICRC embraced a broader mandate to extend protections to noncombatants as far as possible. The organization is considered the custodian of the Geneva Conventions and its role is explicitly recognized in the treaties.

The description 'law of armed conflict' is the preferred choice of military professionals whose historical reference point is the Lieber Code, issued in that same year of 1863. US President Abraham Lincoln commissioned a document formally titled *Instructions for the Government of Armies of the United States in the Field,* General Orders Number 100. It was intended to codify the existing military practice so that soldiers of the Union Army would abide by it. Its author, Francis (Frantz) Lieber, was a German-American jurist and professor at Columbia University who had fought in the Prussian Army against Napoleon. He supported the Union during the Civil War, even though he had lived for many years in South Carolina and his son died in 1862 fighting on the Confederate side.

The two ways of understanding the laws of war share much in common, starting with the basic distinction between *ius ad bellum* – the conditions under which resorting to war is considered legitimate – and *ius in bello* – the types of military strategies and weapons allowed and the treatment of prisoners of war and civilian noncombatants. This fundamental distinction originated with the Catholic Just War tradition centuries ago, but it reflects principles broadly shared across the world's religions. Perhaps more significantly, the ethical tradition of just war became the basis for modern legal restrictions on warfare to which all states are bound.

The United Nations Charter, for example, embodies the principles of *ius ad bellum* in its prohibition on the use of force except for reasons of self-defense or when it is authorized by the Security Council for the preservation of international peace and security. Here the principle of *right authority* comes into play. To justify the use of military force for self-defense, the proper authority is the state itself. This customary norm of international law is reinforced by the United Nations Charter's reference (in Article 51) to 'the inherent right of individual or collective self-defense' that all UN member states enjoy. In situations that affect international peace and security but may not pose direct threats to member states which would justify individual military action in self-defense, the UN Security Council is considered the right authority to sanction the use of force, under Chapter VII of the Charter. The criterion of *reasonable hope* also falls within the scope of the *ius ad bellum*. It refers to the requirement that there be some realistic expectation that the goals of the military operation contemplated will be achieved. It would be difficult to justify harm done to innocent civilians, not to mention the deaths of a country's own soldiers (or even those of the other side), for a hopeless cause. Both right authority and reasonable hope figure prominently in legal and political discussions on such topical issues as 'humanitarian intervention' and preventive war.[1]

Ius in bello principles are reflected in the various Hague and Geneva Conventions which constitute the laws of war and in treaties restricting the use of particular weapons or military practices. Within *ius in bello*, two principles loom large in importance: *distinction* (or *discrimination*) and *proportionality*, which, in turn, is linked to the doctrine of *double effect*. The principle of distinction requires that armed forces distinguish between military and civilian targets, attacking the former and seeking to avoid harming the latter. Double effect is an ethical concept, usually attributed to Thomas Aquinas, with applications to fields ranging from medicine to warfare. It focuses on the actor's intentions in carrying out an act which can have both good and evil consequences (thus, a double effect). In war, killing civilians is considered evil, whereas destroying military facilities or killing soldiers is good. Many attacks produce both effects. Some harm to civilians is expected to occur in all armed conflicts, so killing civilians per se is not illegal or immoral according to just war theory. In order to satisfy the ethical criteria and to adhere to the laws of war, armed forces are not allowed to target civilians directly or to use the deaths of civilians as a means to an end, even if that end – victory – is good. But forswearing the deliberate intention of killing civilians is not enough to excuse or justify their deaths in a military engagement. There must be a reasonable judgment that the good effect – the military benefit – outweighs the evil effect of harm to civilians. That is where the principle of proportionality comes in. Here is a standard, concise definition: 'The loss of life and damage to property incidental to attacks must not be excessive in relation to the concrete and direct military advantage expected to be gained.'[2] That this definition comes from a US Army field manual reinforces the point: Over the centuries, the ethical concepts made their way from just war theory into the body of modern international law, and from there into the rules of engagement which are supposed to govern military practice.

Despite common features, the divergent names for the laws of war imply different points of emphasis. One might hypothesize, for example, that the humanitarian approach reflected in international humanitarian law would privilege civilian welfare over optimal military performance, whereas the military professionals' understanding of the law of armed conflict would favor the exigencies of successful combat and 'military necessity' over the protection of civilians. Like any dichotomy, this one is not fully accurate, but it does seem to reflect the basic tensions underlying the role of law and ethics in international politics, especially as they have surfaced in connection with the war on terror.

In 1939 Edward Hallett Carr, the British historian and analyst of international affairs, described a 'fundamental divergence' in the understanding of international law 'between those who regard law primarily as a branch of ethics, and those who regard it primarily as a vehicle of power'.[3] More than six decades later, the Global War on Terror exposed this divergence as still the fundamental source of disagreement on the purpose of the laws of war. Consider the debate which has emerged over the question, as one observer put it, 'Who owns the rules of war?'[4] Proponents of expanding the scope of humanitarian protections endorse the likeminded efforts of nongovernmental and international organizations and states, particularly in Europe, which have favored limitations on certain weapons and strategies and have sought to hold governments accountable for abuses perpetrated against detainees suspected of conducting or planning terrorist acts. Advocates of this approach invoke pragmatic arguments for pursuing alleged war criminals and scofflaws – deterrence of future abuses, for example – but a sense of moral outrage seems an equally strong motivating force. In the war on terror, that outrage is directed not only against those who undertake terrorist acts but also against those who torture terrorist suspects or wreak havoc on innocent civilians, in an attempt to defeat insurgents.

The opposite position reflects greater concern about the military capabilities of states that are directly engaged in fighting terrorists worldwide and guerrilla insurgencies in places such as Afghanistan and Iraq. The rights of terrorist suspects and of civilians in conflict zones are secondary. Proponents of this position argue that the states that actually practice warfare should set the rules and should not be constrained by other states and organizations that have no direct involvement in military matters. Following Robert Kagan's celebrated generalization that 'Americans are from Mars and Europeans are from Venus', they argue that the pacifically oriented states of the European Union, for example, should not determine the rules that define US military conduct.[5] It is the United States, after all, that bears the lion's share of the burden of defending the world from terrorism. Some suggest that European countries are cynically employing 'lawfare' to limit US power to their benefit. They find it incredible, for example, that the chair of the International Criminal Court's working group tasked with defining the crime of aggression should be the United Nations representative from Liechtenstein, a tiny country that disbanded its eighty-strong army in 1868 and remained neutral in both world wars. In response, defenders of the court might question why the nationality of the working group's chair

should be expected to make any difference to the group's deliberations, when some 150 experts have been involved.[6] And if
nationality did make a difference, what better country to assure
an even-handed approach than one that neither engaged in
aggression nor suffered from it?

Norm Expansion and State Practice

Where the two opposing camps appear to find common
ground is on the influence, to date, of states and organizations
seeking to broaden the scope of civilian protections and to
narrow the legitimate uses of force. They mostly agree that this
influence has been extensive. Proponents of a greater role for
individuals, organizations, and small states celebrate the
emergence of something they call transnational or global civil
society and the increasing ability of 'norm entrepreneurs' to
shape the norms that govern international politics, including
security policy. Opponents observe the same phenomena and
decry the undue influence of unelected individuals, unaccountable organizations and irresponsible governments.

The reality appears to be more ambiguous than either perspective suggests. The rest of this chapter takes up four examples in order to identify the competing interpretations and
illustrate the difficulty of drawing any firm conclusions about
what ultimately is a political process. The examples come from
domains that lawyers would typically separate into two categories, even if to a lay person their names sound rather similar:
international humanitarian law and international human
rights law. The first governs the (violent) behavior of states
towards other states. The second governs the behavior of states
towards individuals, and, in particular, towards their own citizens. The emergence of a body of international law that tells
states how to treat their own citizens already represents the
kind of expansion of norms on behalf of individuals and at the

expense of state sovereignty which many observers associate with the second half of the twentieth century, and particularly the end of the Cold War. The main question that motivates this study is whether the Global War on Terror is likely to put a stop to this apparent trend; more broadly, what are the political dynamics that influence the evolution of international legal and ethical practices? To give a preview of the type of analysis taken up in the rest of the book, the remainder of this chapter introduces four areas where norm entrepreneurs have sought to influence state practice. These include efforts: (1) to limit the impact of war on civilians; (2) to stigmatize and outlaw the practice of torture; (3) to promote international justice for crimes against humanity and war crimes; and (4) to endorse military intervention for humanitarian purposes.

Protecting Civilians in War

Many observers have noted an increasing influence of non-state actors over the last decades, even in realms concerning the most fundamental sovereign prerogatives of states – defense and security, on the one hand, and the treatment of their own citizens, on the other.[7] In the security domain, organizations such as the International Committee of the Red Cross and Human Rights Watch sought to limit the impact of war on civilians.

Perhaps the most striking example, in the years following the end of the Cold War, of the influence of 'global civil society' – for both its admirers and detractors – was the campaign to ban landmines. The effort was spearheaded (to use an inappropriately bellicose metaphor) by nongovernmental organizations. In just five years, grassroots and transnational activists convinced a number of states to sponsor a process that resulted in the 1997 Ottawa Mine Ban Treaty to outlaw the production, sale, and deployment of antipersonnel mines.[8]

Skeptics of a realist bent (who focus on state prerogatives and concerns about security) would point out that the treaty's signatories did not include the world's major producers of landmines, which happened also to be some of the world's leading military powers: the United States, China, Russia. Absent from the list were also countries in particularly war-prone regions: Syria, Egypt, Israel, Iran, Iraq, Saudi Arabia, India, Pakistan.[9] Is this, then, a case that defies the fears (of some) and the hopes (of others) that global civil society will increasingly constrain state prerogatives for making war? Is the mine ban, in fact, simply a feel-good measure with no real impact?

There are two counterarguments to that skeptical view: First, what realist would expect a treaty to come into force in the military sphere despite the opposition of the major states that engage in military operations? In the period 1999 to 2006, 151 countries became parties to the treaty, including Ukraine, whose arsenal of 6.7 million antipersonnel mines constituted the world's fourth largest. During that period nearly forty million stockpiled antipersonnel mines were destroyed, more than 1,100 square kilometers of land were cleared of more than four million antipersonnel mines and one million antivehicle mines, and donors contributed almost two billion dollars to the de-mining efforts.[10] Second, the major powers, with the notable exception of Russia, had by and large abided by the treaty's provisions despite their opposition to them. The United States, as of late 2007, had not used such mines since the 1991 Gulf War, had not exported them since 1992, and had not produced them since 1997. Moreover, the United States was the largest single donor to humanitarian mine-related programs, averaging about 100 million dollars a year for the fiscal years 2004 and 2005, for example.[11]

Only four governments had conducted new mine-laying operations since early 2003: Russia, Myanmar, Nepal, and Georgia. As the result of a policy review in February 2004, the

United States was poised to violate the ban by producing new weapons, by continuing to stockpile old ones, and possibly by deploying landmines in Iraq.[12] In September 2005, the *New York Daily News* reported that the Pentagon was close to making a decision to produce a new landmine. The Defense Department actually requested $1.3 billion for research and production of two new systems (between fiscal years 2005 and 2011). Although this was evidently a setback for efforts to 'universalize' the treaty, the Pentagon's behavior nevertheless reflected the influence of the anti-mine norms that produced the Ottawa accord. How so? As the newspaper put it, 'underscoring the unpopularity of the devices, defense officials working on the program, called Spider, decline to call the weapon a land mine, opting instead for generic descriptions such as "networked munitions"'.[13] In 2002, the Pentagon agency known as the Project Manager for Mines, Countermine and Demolitions had already changed its name to Project Manager Close Combat Systems, to avoid the obvious association with a weapon that much of the world had declared illegal. So officials in the Pentagon apparently recognized a normative stigma against landmines, at least enough not to want to say out loud that they intended to produce new ones. Such an action would nevertheless be completely legal, because the United States never signed the Mine Ban Treaty. Reinforcing the stigma and bolstering the status of the Ottawa Mine Ban, US legislators sought to prevent the United States from developing any new weapons that fit the treaty's definition of a mine.[14]

Despite uncertainty about the staying power of the emerging taboo against landmines, the Ottawa Treaty would appear to be a case where norms shaped practice, rather than one where prevailing practice became codified into law. And it would contradict the realist expectation, described by E. H. Carr, which characterizes international morality and law as 'the product of dominant nations or groups of nations'.[15] In this case, we have norms promoted by nongovernmental organizations and small and medium powers. There is even a possibility that the prohibition against mines could attain the status of customary law. In that case, even the states that did not sign the treaty would be expected to abide by the ban.[16]

In the wake of the success of the mine-ban campaign, activist groups and sympathetic governments set their sights on further restrictions – namely on cluster munitions. The weapons, when used in populated areas, cause indiscriminate harm to civilians, and the 'bomblets' that the weapons disperse can remain dangerous long after their initial use. In that respect they resemble landmines as 'explosive remnants of war', and opponents have sought to limit or ban them accordingly. The use of cluster bombs by US forces in Afghanistan and Iraq and by the Israeli Defense Forces in Lebanon in the summer of 2006 called the world's attention to their effect on civilians and gave the campaign a boost.

In cases such as those of campaigns for banning landmines or for limiting the use of cluster bombs, human rights groups are seeking to expand the normative and legal constraints on the use of military power beyond what existing law explicitly provides. They represent the school of thought which views the laws of war as intended to broaden the scope of humanitarian protections rather than simply to serve the interests or to reflect the practices of states that engage in warfare.

In 2005, the ICRC compiled a 5,000-page study identifying 161 rules governing warfare – rules which, in its view, had attained customary law status: each state was obliged to obey them, even if it had not signed specific treaties agreeing to do so.[17] The judgment about what constitutes customary law is supposed to be based in part on the actual practice of states, but it can also include factors such as predominant legal opinion from specialists who do not represent governments.[18] Thus this sphere of law-making raises the possibility that prevailing legal norms will diverge from the actual practice of war-making states.

Despite the apparent momentum achieved by successes such as the Ottawa Treaty, other efforts to limit warfare have fared worse. Most notably, the largest transnational peace movement the world has ever seen failed to halt the US-led invasion of Iraq.[19] In the wake of 11 September, states have sought to reassert their prerogatives over non-state actors, even nonviolent ones, if the latter seem to pose a threat to state security or sovereignty. Throughout the world, from Chechnya to Somalia to the Philippines, states have engaged in armed conflict against separatists and insurgents, justifying their actions as part of a global war on terror. Could it be that *in bello* restrictions on state practice – those governing the means of warfare – are more amenable to the influence of norm entrepreneurs than *ad bellum* restrictions on states' decisions to go to war? Yet, even on the side of means, we do not observe consistent progress towards civilian protection. The ICRC codification of customary laws of war, for example, and Human Rights Watch's close monitoring of US targeting practices have not prevented the deaths of hundreds of thousands of civilians in Afghanistan, Iraq, and Lebanon. Regarding both ends and means, the jury is still out on whether the war on terror will weaken existing norms and set new, more permissive standards, based on state practice, or whether popular reactions to the way states wage that war will lead to further restrictions.

Stigmatizing Torture

Treatment of a state's own citizens or subjects would appear to be a sine qua non of sovereignty. Yet, when it comes to torture, one observes deliberate efforts by individuals and groups to influence state practice towards its stigmatization and ultimate eradication. The efforts have extended over the course of decades, or even centuries. Once an accepted method of interrogation and punishment during the Middle Ages and up to modern times (for example, giving suspects 'the third degree' in US domestic police practices), torture became an internationally recognized crime against humanity by the end of the twentieth century. Starting in the 1970s, nongovernmental organizations such as Amnesty International played an increasingly active role in shaming governments that practiced torture, for instance the military dictatorships in Latin America, and the campaigns of such organizations in favor of human rights have contributed to the peaceful overthrow of those regimes in favor of democracy. Observing such developments, some scholars have identified a 'justice cascade', a 'rapid shift towards recognizing the legitimacy of human rights norms and an increase in international and regional action to effect compliance with those norms'.[20]

In the US war on terror, the moral and legal acceptability of torture – once, seemingly, the most settled of issues – has become a subject of public discussion, as high US officials endorsed the practice in all but name. A question of basic human rights became captive to security concerns, as the efforts of nongovernmental organizations, particularly on behalf of detainees held at Guantánamo, triggered a backlash. Prominent US political figures, for example, criticized the ICRC for having 'failed to recognize the changing nature of war' and for claiming 'that the United States has obligations under international humanitarian law that go far beyond the obligations that the US government recognizes under its ratified treaties'. In doing so, they seemed to reject the very notion of customary law.[21] Key voices within the administration of George W. Bush more explicitly suggested that compliance with the Geneva Conventions was a matter of the president's own prerogative, not a legal requirement. One Bush administration official branded as un-American the US lawyers who provided *pro bono* legal counsel to the detainees, and took a leaf from the repertoire of social movements by urging a boycott of the corporate law firms that employed them.[22]

Pursuing International Justice

International justice is a domain where norm entrepreneurs have worked for many years to shift state practice. Transnational activists played a major role in two particular initiatives intended to bring to justice individuals guilty of mass atrocities and war crimes. The first was universal jurisdiction; the second was the International Criminal Court, based on the Rome Statute of 1998. The practice of universal jurisdiction, considered part of the 'justice cascade', appeared to make great strides during the last years of the twentieth century, propelled as it was by the transnational collaboration of lawyers, judges, victims' families, and human rights activists. Universal jurisdiction allows for the prosecution of crimes which are, in the words of one authority, 'so heinous, so potentially disruptive of international peace, and so difficult for any one state to adequately prosecute, that all states have the right to try anyone accused of them'.[23] The most high-profile case was that of Chilean General Augusto Pinochet, whose extradition from England was sought by Spain in order to make him face charges of genocide and torture for the reign of terror he carried out under the military dictatorship that began with the overthrow of the Chilean government in 1973. The House of Lords agreed to extradition and overruled Pinochet's claim of immunity for the crimes committed as part of his official duties as head of state. The Lords argued that the crime of torture is not subject to such immunity and that, moreover, as a party to the Torture Convention of 1984, Britain had an obligation, not merely an option, to pursue allegations of torture.[24] The British government ultimately decided, however, to allow Pinochet to return to Chile for reasons of health, but the Spanish courts continued to pursue other cases related to human rights abuses in Latin America.

The dawn of the twenty-first century saw the heyday of international justice, perhaps best represented by Belgium's law on universal jurisdiction. Human rights activists used it to seek the prosecution of Hissan Habré, a former Chadian dictator, from his refuge in Senegal, while others pursued figures ranging from former Israeli Prime Minister Ariel Sharon (for the 1982 and Shatila massacres) to US Generals Norman Schwarzkopf and Tommy Franks (for their roles in the 1991 Iraq War and in the 1999 Kosovo War, respectively). Eventually, Belgium narrowed the scope of the law considerably, partly in response to US threats to remove NATO headquarters from Brussels.

Some have argued that the 'justice cascade' against human rights abuses continued in countries undergoing democratizing transitions from repressive regimes, despite the war on terror.[25] If so, efforts to apply the same standards to accused war criminals in the states prosecuting that war (even the ostensibly mature democracies) fared far worse. The commitment to universal jurisdiction seemed to lose steam, even as the International Criminal Court cautiously came into operation. A transnational effort to bring Donald Rumsfeld and other US officials to account for torture, for example, foundered in April 2007, when a German court dismissed the case on the grounds that the US judicial system should handle the matter. A month earlier, a US district court had already declared that, because 'detaining and interrogating enemy aliens were the kinds of conduct the defendants were employed to perform', Rumsfeld and the others would not be prosecuted for torture carried out in the course of detention and interrogation.[26] The war on terror seems to have called into question a precedent that some believed was established at Nuremberg – that of holding superiors accountable for the actions of their subordinates.[27]

As far as the International Criminal Court is concerned, a key question is the US role. The United States, under the administration of William Clinton, signed the Rome Statute with some ambivalence, but never ratified it. The Bush administration 'unsigned' the treaty and negotiated bilateral deals with many countries (under threat of eliminating economic aid) to extract commitments from them that they would never bring US citizens before the court. Contrary to expectations, the administration did, however, cooperate with the court on some issues, such as the genocide in Darfur.[28]

Humanitarian Intervention

With the pursuit of universal jurisdiction and promotion of the International Criminal Court, transnational activists issued a fundamental challenge to state sovereignty and to prevailing state practice, in the interest of punishing human rights abuses. Some activists focused their attention on the prevention of such abuses, if necessary by military means. Under the rubric Responsibility to Protect, they urged the United Nations to endorse *humanitarian intervention*, the use of international military force 'where a population is suffering serious harm, as a result of internal war, insurgency, repression or state failure, and the state in question is unwilling or unable to halt or avert it'.[29] A high-level commission appointed by then UN Secretary General Kofi Annan endorsed the R2P agenda, as it was becoming known, and in a 2005 report prepared for the General Assembly Annan himself urged states to embrace the 'emerging norm of the Responsibility to Protect'.[30]

The issue of humanitarian intervention is different from the other three domains we have considered. In this case, norm

entrepreneurs were not trying to restrict an existing state practice (military behavior causing harm to civilians, physical coercion and torture, or protection of alleged criminals from
international justice). Instead, they sought to promote a new
state practice – military intervention for humanitarian purposes – and to enshrine a new norm, the 'responsibility to protect'. Ironically, even when the activists thought they had
won – as when states embraced the rhetoric of R2P – the victory was a pyrrhic one. High-profile cases of genocide, such as
in Darfur, generated concern, but little serious action on the
part of the major powers; lower-profile massacres in the
Central African Republic and mass sexual violence in Côte
d'Ivoire received less attention. Yet, with the war on terror, the
US government appeared surprisingly open to some of the
activists' arguments, as the Bush administration sought to
adopt the language of human rights to provide a humanitarian
justification for its military actions. In defense of the war in
Iraq, and even in Afghanistan, the administration articulated a
rationale for military force that echoed the rhetoric of the R2P
campaign and added a security dimension – the need to
engage in preventive wars to stem the proliferation of weapons
of mass destruction.

The subsequent invasion of Iraq garnered the support of
many American liberal internationalists who welcomed the
overthrow of a brutal dictator. Confusion and disagreement
over the war and subsequent occupation undermined any
notion of 'global civil society' premised on the assumption
of homogeneity and transnational cooperation. The simple
dichotomy of state practice versus norm expansion founders
in the case of humanitarian intervention. The expansion of a
norm (the responsibility to protect) has contributed to a state
practice (preventive war) that makes many of the original
norm entrepreneurs uneasy. Humanitarian aid organizations
faced a crisis in their relationship with the United States.

Embraced by then Secretary of State Colin Powell in 2001 as 'a force multiplier for us' and as 'an important part of our combat team', they later came under terrorist attack in Iraq, where even traditionally neutral and inviolable organizations such as the ICRC and UN were viewed as part of the US-led occupation force.[31] As Chapter 5 describes, some activists have criticized the United States for politicizing humanitarian aid, while other observers have suggested that NGOs cannot avoid taking sides in the war against terror.

This chapter has identified several areas where the end of the Cold War has witnessed efforts intended to enhance human rights and security – to limit the impact of war, to eradicate torture, to bring international criminals to justice, and to save victims of atrocities and genocide. These areas exhibit a complicated relationship between the efforts of norm entrepreneurs and the practice of states in shaping the laws and norms that govern international behavior. The overall impression is that the war on terror has led to serious setbacks in many of these domains. The matters discussed in the next chapters are no less complicated. Governments disagree among themselves on some of the key legal and ethical issues posed by the threat of Islamist terrorism and by the response of its main antagonist, the United States. Within countries, legal specialists and philosophers rarely express unanimity of views. The purpose of the rest of the book is to examine some of the most controversial questions, to offer a summary of the main contending views, and to make some assessment about the likely evolution of norms and state practice.

CHAPTER TWO

Terrorism: Definitional Controversies

This chapter addresses historical controversies over the definition of terrorism and shows how states and international
organizations have sought to resolve them. Traditionally, states
have tended to portray themselves as the main targets of terrorism and have sought to include non-state status as part of
the very definition of a terrorist. Such definitions privilege
state prerogatives and de-legitimate recourse to violence by
non-state actors for purposes of political change – secessionist
or 'national liberation' movements, for example. They also
appear to excuse behavior, conducted by states or their agents,
which would seem to fit commonsensical definitions of terrorism – such as massacres of unarmed peasants suspected of
sympathy to a guerrilla insurgency. Even among states, there
are disagreements about which non-state actors deserve the
epithet 'terrorist' – reflected in the aphorism that one state's
terrorist is another state's freedom fighter. Is it futile, then, to
try to define terrorism as a step towards limiting it?

Few would disagree that coping with terrorist organizations
that operate globally requires a coordinated international
response and cooperation. It is all the more remarkable, then,
that states have had such difficulty cooperating enough to produce even a common definition of terrorism. One problem
that bedevils efforts to agree on a definition concerns the scope
of the term. Virtually all definitions of terrorism identify innocent civilian victims as being among the targets of violence.
Disagreements come into play as to whether 'terrorism' is still

the right word to use if the *victims* are government representatives, either civilian or military, or if the *perpetrators* are government agents, including, for example, armed forces. If states do not agree about who is a terrorist, then they will not cooperate in putting suspects on trial or in extraditing them for trial elsewhere. One state's terrorist could receive safe haven as another state's freedom fighter.[1]

Historical Precursors

Many of the disagreements about the definition of terrorism date to the origins of the phenomenon itself and are reflected in the etymology of the ancient terms we still use: zealots, assassins, and thugs.[2] These words entered the English lexicon so long ago that many are unaware of their foreign origins, or that they were essentially synonyms for different types of violent actors who would today fall into the broadest category of 'terrorist'. Examining these three groups suggests the elements that we might or might not want to include in a definition of terrorist. These particular groups, for example, were motivated to varying degrees by religious belief – Jewish, Muslim, and Hindu respectively – but they typically attacked the *political* authorities who stood in the way of achieving their religious vision. Secular, nonreligious terrorism also has a long pedigree, and we shall review some examples of that as well.

    Of the three groups, the Jewish Zealots or Sicarii (from the Latin word 'sica' for 'dagger') were the earliest. They actively opposed Roman control of the Holy Land in the decades before the destruction of the Temple at Jerusalem in 70 CE. Although the Zealots' main target was Roman rule, they deliberately harmed their fellow Jews, seeking to provoke them to rebellion. Thus they murdered innocent civilians as well as political and military officials. The Assassins, too, committed violence against fellow Muslims who did not share their sect's beliefs. They favored a literal reading of the Qur'an's prohibition to take up the sword against co-religionists, and managed to get around it by using daggers instead (like the Sicarii). The Thugs chose *only* fellow Hindus as their victims, to offer them as sacrifices to the goddess Kali. Unlike the other two groups, who pursued political goals, the Thugs appear to have been motivated mainly by their religious beliefs. Terrorism for these groups was a weapon of the weak, targeted against the official authorities. They used innocent civilian deaths as a means to achieve their ends – political or religious change.[3]

A more recent historical precursor to contemporary terrorism dates to the second half of the nineteenth century and to the early twentieth century. Its motivations were primarily political, reflecting the major movements of the era: socialism, fascism, nationalism, anarchism. The targets of political violence were typically leaders. In the half-century following the assassination of US President Abraham Lincoln in 1865, two more US presidents were killed, along with a Russian tsar, an Austro-Hungarian empress; Italian, Portuguese, Serbian, and Greek kings and queens; prime ministers, interior ministers, and foreign ministers from Spain, Germany, and Finland; and – perhaps most consequentially – the Austro-Hungarian archduke, whose assassination sparked the outbreak of World War I (see Table 2.1).

Definitions of Terrorism

Given the amount of political violence directed against state leaders, it is not surprising that the early efforts to define terrorism as an international crime identified *states* as the ultimate target. This is also consistent with the view that state prerogatives determine the nature of international law. In

Table 2.1 A very partial list of successful assassinations, 1865–1922*	
Year	**Victim**
1865	US President Abraham Lincoln
1880	US President James Garfield
1881	Russian Tsar Alexander II
1898	Empress Elizabeth of Austria–Hungary
1901	US President William McKinley
1901	Italian King Umberto I
1903	Serbian King Alexander I and Queen Draga
1904	Russian Interior Minister Viacheslav Plehve
1905	Russian Grand Duke Sergei Alexandrovich
1908	Portuguese King Carlos I
1912	Spanish Prime Minister José Canalejas y Méndez
1913	King George I of Greece
1914	Archduke Franz Ferdinand of Austria–Hungary
1921	Spanish Prime Minister Eduardo Dato Iradier
1922	Finnish Minister of Internal Affairs Heikki Ritavuori
1922	German Foreign Minister Walter Rathenau

* For a more comprehensive list of attempts and successes, see
http://www.caslon.com.au/assassinationsnote4.htm (accessed 18 August 2007)

1937 the League of Nations proposed the following definition of terrorism, which was never officially adopted: 'All criminal acts directed against a State and intended or calculated to create a state of terror in the minds of particular persons or a group of persons or the general public.'[4] The current official definition of the US Department of Defense maintains the focus on the state: 'The calculated use of unlawful violence to inculcate fear, intended to coerce or to intimidate governments or societies in the pursuit of goals that are generally political, religious, or ideological.' The department's definition of a terrorist is quite broad – 'an individual who commits an act or acts of violence or threatens violence in pursuit of political, religious, or ideological objectives' – but it misses some features that other definitions prominently include. There is, for example, no requirement that the individual be part of a larger organization, that the individual's acts actually result in any violence, or apparently that they even be premeditated or planned.[5]

A curious feature of the definitions offered by the League of Nations and by the Pentagon is that neither of them suggests that the victims of terrorist violence need be innocent civilians. Judging by the focus on intimidating governments, one might infer that the definition's authors had in mind primarily government officials as victims of terrorism. In the case of the US Department of Defense, at least some military officers seemed to have themselves in mind as potential targets. In a lesson plan prepared for instructors of the US Navy Reserve Officers Training Corps (NROTC), for instance, the department's official definition of terrorism was followed by an example: the 1981 kidnapping, by the Italian Red Brigades, of US Army Brigadier General James Dozier from his residence in Verona. Dozier was rescued by the Italian police after forty-two days. Other officials were not so lucky; these included the Italian politician Aldo Moro, whom the Red Brigades kidnapped and murdered. Extremists of the left and right in Italy were responsible for the murders of many innocent civilians along with those of government and military officials during the 1970s and 1980s, but it was the kidnapping of a US military officer that was, understandably, expected to 'gain attention' from the cadets of the NROTC classroom, in the words of the lesson plan.[6]

In contrast to the US Defense Department's definition, the one used by the US Central Intelligence Agency and by the State Department until 2005 emphasized noncombatants as the main targets. It adopted the language of the relevant US domestic legislation: 'The term "terrorism" means premeditated, politically motivated violence perpetrated against noncombatant targets by subnational groups or clandestine agents, usually intended to influence an audience.' This definition would not exclude General Dozier, because 'the term "noncombatant" is interpreted to include, in addition to civilians, military personnel who at the time of the incident are unarmed and/or not on duty'.[7] It might, however, call into question the designation of the suicide attack against the USS Cole in October 2000, in which seventeen sailors died, as a terrorist act – simply because a guided missile destroyer belonging to the US Navy is not a noncombatant target.

A particularly controversial aspect of the debate on definitions of terrorism concerns the question whether the states themselves, or their agents, should be said to engage in terrorism. If the victims of state violence are innocent civilians, many argue, then the designation 'terrorist' is appropriate. In 1792, in what was perhaps the first use of the term 'terrorist' in English, Edmund Burke employed it as an epithet against a state leader – namely Robespierre, the French revolutionary, who by that stage had assumed the powers of the French state, now a republic, to impose thousands of deaths by guillotine. Robespierre defended what he himself called a regime of terror imposed upon fellow citizens of his own country. He was only one in a long line of terrorist leaders. Mass killings perpetrated to instill fear and enforce discipline were also key elements of the twentieth-century dictatorships of Hitler, Stalin, Mao, and Pol Pot (among others). Historians of the Soviet Union call the second half of the 1930s – the period of maximum regime-sponsored carnage – the Great Terror. The murders carried out by state-linked 'death squads', which killed civilians suspected of disloyalty to the regime, caused charges of government-sponsored terrorism to be brought against military dictatorships in El Salvador and Guatemala during the 1980s; but the practice was widespread in many parts of the world. Clearly, states engage in behavior that, common sense suggests, could be called terrorism. In these cases, the violence was directed against the subjects or citizens of the states carrying out the acts. Under those circumstances, one can understand why the governments that engage in the practices in question would resist including such behavior in an internationally endorsed definition of terrorism.

What about cases where states deliberately kill innocent civilians of other states, as for example in the course of a war, or during military occupation? As we have seen in Chapter 1, just war theory and the laws of war expect civilians to die in wartime, and only deem their deaths illegal if they are intended or if the extent of unintended civilian damage is disproportionate to the military gain. The era of European colonialism witnessed many deliberate attacks against civilians. Especially when faced with insurgencies, colonial armies would inflict great harm on members of the civilian population, whether in an effort to isolate them from the fighters (frequently by forcing them into concentration camps) or by way of deliberately punishing them for suspected support of the rebellion.[8] Should these practices be called terrorism?

In some cases, the colonial powers themselves used the term 'terrorism' to describe what they were doing. The French in Algeria, for example, referred to their methods for combating the terror tactics of the Front de Libération Nationale (FLN) as 'counter-terrorism' – by which they meant, in particular, the use of death squads such as the Organisation Armée Secrète, which carried out bombings and murders of civilians to avenge attacks of the FLN and to create a state of panic and demoralization among their supporters.[9] The Geneva Conventions of 1949 and their additional protocols signed in 1977 prohibit the collective punishment of populations under military occupation and employ the term 'terrorism' in relation to this kind of action: 'Collective penalties and likewise all measures of intimidation or of terrorism are prohibited.'[10] The inspiration for this prohibition came from the atrocities inflicted upon civilian populations under occupation by Nazi Germany and Imperial Japan during World War II. Critics of Israel cite the use of the word 'terrorism' in this sense in the Geneva Conventions to justify charges to the effect that the Israeli authorities engage in terrorism when they destroy the homes of convicted Palestinian terrorists in the occupied territories.[11]

Terrorism in War

During the twentieth century, the largest numbers of civilians killed directly by military action were victims of aerial bombardment. During World War II, the Allies destroyed scores of German and Japanese cities by dropping incendiary explosives that caused vast firestorms and killed tens of thousands of people. Not surprisingly, the strategy became known as terror-bombing. The early theorists of air power, such as Giulio Douhet, Billy Mitchell, and Hugh Trenchard, writing soon after World War I, expected that noncombatants would be the primary targets of air attack in the next war. 'The brutal but inescapable conclusion we must draw', wrote Douhet, was that 'in the face of the technical development of aviation today, in case of war the strongest army we can deploy . . . and the strongest navy we can dispose . . . will provide no effective defense against determined efforts . . . to bomb our cities . . . How could a country go on living and working under this constant threat, oppressed by the nightmare of imminent destruction and death?'[12]

Much as Alfred Nobel expected that his invention of dynamite would make wars too terrible to fight, so did Douhet naively anticipate that targeting civilians would shorten a war and that wars themselves would consequently become more humane. 'The more rapid and terrifying the arms are,' he predicted, 'the faster they will reach vital centers and the more deeply they will affect moral resistance. Hence the more civilized war will become.'[13] World War II disproved Douhet's predictions, as both sides fought on for years despite the devastation that aerial bombardment wrought on cities. Even before Germany initiated the war through its invasion of Poland in 1939, German air forces had been bombing civilian targets in Spain, in support of the fascist armies of Francisco Franco. The 1937 attack on Guernica is the best-known example, because it was commemorated in Pablo Picasso's famous painting.

The laws of war relevant to aerial bombardment were rather undeveloped at the outbreak of World War II. The Hague Convention, adopted in 1899 and revised in 1907, prohibited 'attack or bombardment of towns, villages, habitations or buildings which are not defended' (Article 25) and required the attackers to warn the relevant authorities on the other side in advance (Article 26) and to take all necessary steps 'to spare as far as possible edifices devoted to religion, art, science, and charity, hospitals, and places where the sick and wounded are collected, provided they are not used at the same time for military purposes' (Article 27).

The condition that a population center be undefended in order to be spared bombardment left a rather large loophole, as the presence of any troops or military facilities might annul it. Nevertheless, the onus against the intentional killing of civilians was evident in the reactions of British and US leaders to the German air campaign of 1939 and the Japanese attacks in Manchuria. British Prime Minister Winston Churchill, for example, condemned Hitler's bombing of Warsaw and Rotterdam as 'a new and odious form of attack', and vowed that his government would not 'bomb nonmilitary objectives, no matter what the policy of the German Government may be'.

The US government issued a statement in response to Japan's bombing campaign, reinforcing its view that 'any general bombing of an extensive area wherein there resides a large populace engaged in peaceful pursuits is unwarranted and contrary to the principles of law and humanity'. At the outbreak of World War II, President Franklin Roosevelt invoked both the legal prohibition of the Hague Conventions and the broader moral principle of civilian immunity when he addressed 'an urgent appeal to every government which may be engaged in hostilities publicly to affirm its determination that its armed forces shall, in no event and in no circumstances, undertake the bombardment from the air of civilian populations or of unfortified cities'.[14]

Although not much appreciated at the time or since, the criticism of Germany's bombing of civilian targets reflected considerable hypocrisy on Churchill's part. During the period 1919–22 Churchill served as Britain's Secretary of State for War, Secretary of State for Air, and Secretary of State for the Colonies, being tasked with enforcing order among the people who resisted foreign rule. One of the tools he advocated was aerial bombardment of tribal areas by poison gas. It is not unreasonable to say that Britain effectively invented terror-bombing in the 1920s, in an effort to control unruly tribes in Iraq, as well as in India and Afghanistan. In February 1920, Churchill wrote to Hugh Trenchard, Chief of the Air Staff, recommending the use of air power in Iraq, including 'the provision of some kind of asphyxiating bombs calculated to cause disablement of some kind but not death, for use in preliminary operations against turbulent tribes'. Churchill insisted the gas would cause 'only discomfort or illness, but not death', even though he received reports that it could induce blindness and 'kill children and sickly persons, more especially as the people against whom we intend to use it have no medical knowledge with which to supply antidotes'. He rejected such considerations as reflecting 'the prejudices of those who do not think clearly' and claimed not to 'understand this squeamishness about the use of gas. I am strongly in favour of using poison gas against uncivilised tribes.' In the event, the British used aerial bombardment against many villages in Kurdistan and gas (although not delivered by air) against Iraqi rebels – with, in Churchill's words, 'excellent moral effect'. With Churchill's blessing, Trenchard sought to use the Iraqi campaign's results to boost the standing of his branch of the armed services, submitting a report to the cabinet on 'The development of air control in Iraq'.[15]

The British and other colonial powers appeared to hold two standards regarding the murder of civilians by air – one for 'civilized' peoples, and another for everybody else. At the 1932 Disarmament Conference, the British delegation was willing to restrict aerial bombardment, but not 'the use of such machines as are necessary for police purposes in outlying places', that is, in the colonies. As Prime Minister David Lloyd George put it, without hiding the racist attitudes at the core of British policy, 'we insisted on the right to bomb niggers!'[16]

Whatever official opposition to 'civilized' Germany's terror-bombing the British and US authorities had voiced at the start of World War II, it diminished as the Allies came to depend on air power as a key element of their own war strategy. From initially forswearing deliberate attacks on civilians, both governments came increasingly close to justifying the intentional targeting of an enemy population in order to destroy its morale. A 1943 joint US–British operational plan, for example, envisioned 'the progressive destruction and dislocation of the German military, industrial, and economic system, and the undermining of the morale of the German people to a point where their capacity for armed resistance is fatally weakened'. That same year, Churchill reported to the British public that 'the almost total systematic destruction of many of the centers of German war effort continues on a greater scale and at a greater pace. The havoc wrought is indescribable and the effect upon the German war production in all its forms . . . is matched by that wrought upon the life and economy of the whole of that guilty organization.'[17] Otherwise known for the elegance and clarity of his speech, Churchill here leaves ambiguous what he intends by 'that guilty organization'. One plausibly infers that he means the whole German nation, without taking account of the possibility that some people (babies, at least?) may be quite innocent. The firebombing of cities such as Hamburg, Dresden, and Tokyo, with perhaps a hundred thousand victims each, made no distinctions. Nor did the atomic bombings of Hiroshima and Nagasaki – unusual not for the number of victims, but for the fact that those victims were killed by a single bomb dropped over each city.

If the strategic bombing of World War II represented a nadir in protection of civilians from deliberate harm, the wars of the early post-war period did not show much improvement – not least because they were conducted by the same people who had directed the air campaigns during the war. General Curtis LeMay, for example, was the primary architect of the firebombing and atomic bombing strategy against Japan. In 1949 he was appointed first head of the Strategic Air Command of the newly independent US Air Force (it had previously been part of the Army). During the Korean War which broke out in June 1950, LeMay emerged as a leading advocate of firebombing, as he recalled in an oral history interview, and he seemed almost proud of the fact that the strategy killed many civilians: 'We slipped a note kind of under the door into the Pentagon and said, "Look, let us go up there . . . and burn down five of the biggest towns in North Korea – and they're not very big – and that ought to stop it." Well, the answer to that was four or five screams – "You'll kill a lot of non-combatants", and "[i]t's too horrible"'. 'Yet', as LeMay accurately remembered, 'over a period three years or so . . . we burned down *every* town in North Korea and South Korea, too.' Indeed, a 1952 US war plan for Korea explicitly emphasized damage to civilians as a goal, stating that 'whenever possible attacks will be scheduled against targets of military significance so situated that their destruction will have a deleterious effect upon the morale of the civilian population'.[18]

Such terror-bombing continued well into the post-war period. The US war in Vietnam saw, in the most conservative estimates, tens of thousands of civilians die as a result of 'carpet bombing' by B-52 bombers. US forces used napalm deliberately to set fire to forests and cropland. The United States dropped more tons of explosives on North and South Vietnam than all the bombs used by all of the belligerents during World War II – including the two atomic bombs. The Soviet Union in its decade-long war in Afghanistan and post-Soviet Russia in its conflict in Chechnya employed mass area bombing to terrorize civilians.[19]

The most direct association of terror with bombing came at the dawn of the nuclear age. Thomas Schelling, the influential economist and nuclear strategist, described the atomic bombs dropped on Hiroshima and Nagasaki as 'weapons of terror and shock', intended more for their political effect than for any military one. The bombs 'represented violence against the country itself and not mainly an attack on Japan's material strength'.[20] During the Cold War, nuclear deterrence was premised on the fear of mass killings among the civilian population. Albert Wohlstetter, Schelling's colleague at the Rand Corporation and later a mentor to Paul Wolfowitz at the University of Chicago, famously described the nuclear arms race between the United States and the Soviet Union as 'the delicate balance of terror'.[21]

Nuclear deterrence – seeking to forestall an act by threat of nuclear retaliation – only works by invoking the fear of mass civilian casualties. Yet political and military authorities claim to uphold the principle of noncombatant immunity by insisting that their *intention* is not to kill civilians. If the early US plans for war against the Soviet Union, for example, entailed attacking Moscow with seventy atomic bombs, Defense Department officials would insist that the targets – military, economic, and political – were strictly related to the Soviet ability to prosecute the war. The United States did not target civilians per se, even though millions of them would die – and the expectation of those deaths would be presumably what was supposed to deter Soviet aggression. Focusing on intentions rather than behavior serves as a way of reconciling putative American values with actions that clearly violate them.[22]

If one focuses on *consequences* rather than intentions, the distinction begins to blur between terrorism committed by non-state actors and violence perpetrated against civilians by states at war. The eminent US historian Howard Zinn made this point in objecting to the common distinction drawn between the deliberate killing of civilians by suicide bombers, for example, and the unintentional killing of civilians as 'collateral damage' in aerial bombardment:

> These words are misleading because they assume an action is either 'deliberate' or 'unintentional'. There is something in between, for which the word is 'inevitable'. If you engage in an action, like aerial bombing, in which you cannot possibly distinguish between combatants and civilians (as a former Air Force bombardier, I will attest to that), the deaths of civilians are inevitable, even if not 'intentional.' Does that difference exonerate you morally?

Zinn concludes that 'the terrorism of the suicide bomber and the terrorism of aerial bombardment are indeed morally equivalent. To say otherwise (as either side might) is to give one moral superiority over the other, and thus serve to perpetuate the horrors of our time.'[23] Proponents of just war theory would point out that the principles of double effect and proportionality provide a way for an evil action (the killing of innocent civilians) to be foreseen, but also to appear morally acceptable if the (good) military benefit outweighs the civilian harm. If civilian harm becomes the *means* to an end (such as victory in the war) rather than an unintended, if foreseen, consequence, the distinction between suicide terrorism and the terror-bombing of population centers does appear to vanish.

For all the commonsense plausibility of equating the terror-inducing behavior of states at war with the atrocities carried out by non-state actors, one should not be surprised to find that the states themselves reject the equation. If a consensus definition of terrorism is a prerequisite for international cooperation, it is not likely to prohibit terroristic acts of war.

Political Violence by Non-State Actors: Is it always Terrorism?

Michael Walzer, in his classic study, *Just and Unjust Wars*, devoted a chapter to terrorism. He sought to apply the just war tradition, what he called the 'war convention', to the topic of political violence by non-state actors. He started with a premise that seems less popular today – at least among representatives of states – than it did when he was writing in the mid-1970s, namely that some forms of political violence by individuals and groups are morally justified.

Walzer's definition of terrorism contains a concept which is rarely found in the myriad other definitions proposed: *randomness*. Indeed an internet search of the terms 'terrorism' and 'random' will turn up hundreds more references to a publisher of books about terrorism that has Random as part of its name than to the word *random* used in connection with victims of terrorism. Yet for Walzer 'randomness is the crucial feature of terrorist activity'. Terrorism 'in the strict sense' is 'the random murder of innocent people'. Walzer draws on just war theory for the principle of a distinction between combatants and non-combatants or civilians. If individuals and groups carry out violence for political purposes which is targeted against representatives of a (presumably repressive) state, and if they deliberately seek to avoid doing harm to innocent civilians, they should not be called terrorists. Indeed, Walzer believes that such individuals are following 'a political code first worked out in the second half of the nineteenth century and roughly analogous to the laws of war worked out at the same time'. Walzer suggests that 'adherence to this code did not prevent revolutionary militants from being called terrorists, but in fact the violence they committed bore little resemblance to contemporary terrorism. It was not random murder but assassination, and it involved the drawing of a line that we will have little difficulty recognizing as the political parallel of the line that marks off combatants from noncombatants.' Walzer summarizes his moral judgment as follows:

> The war convention and the political code are structurally similar, and the distinction between officials and citizens parallels that between soldiers and civilians (though the two are not the same). What lies behind them both, I think, and lends them plausibility, is the moral difference between aiming and not aiming – or, more accurately, between aiming at particular people because of things they have done or are doing, and aiming at whole groups of people, indiscriminately, because of who they are.

For Walzer, 'the first kind of aiming' – political assassination – 'is appropriate to a limited struggle directed against regimes and policies', whereas the second – indiscriminate attacks against civilians – 'reaches beyond all limits'.[24]

As is appropriate in a study that pays homage to the case-by-case analysis of the Christian casuists who developed just war theory, Walzer offers a couple of examples of the morally acceptable behavior of people he insists should not be called terrorists. He writes, for example, of the Irish Republican Army's campaign of bombings carried out in Britain on behalf of an independent Ireland in 1938–9. On one occasion a militant carrying a bomb on his bicycle to blow up the power station in Coventry got lost and abandoned the bomb just as it was about to explode. It killed five innocent civilians, to the horror and embarrassment of the IRA militants who planned the attack.

Walzer describes an earlier case of the attempted assassination in February 1905 of Grand Duke Sergei, the brother of the Russian tsar Aleksandr III. The story of Ivan Kaliaev is especially apt for posing ethical questions about unjust regimes and about the difference between assassination and terrorism. For these reasons Albert Camus used it as the basis of his 1949 play, *Les Justes*. Kaliaev was a member of the military wing of the Russian Socialist Revolutionary (SR) Party who, disguised as a peasant, was poised to throw a bomb into the carriage of the grand duke as the latter made his way to a performance at the Bolshoi Theater. As he was about to toss the bomb, Kaliaev noticed that Sergei was traveling with his wife and had two small children on his lap, and he decided not to go ahead with the plan. Even though they acknowledged that he had put himself and the organization at risk, Kaliaev's comrades all agreed that he had done the right thing by not killing the children. Kaliaev managed to assassinate the grand duke a couple of days later. He was captured immediately, put on trial, and executed by hanging. On the hundredth anniversary of Kaliaev's death, a Russian writer described him as a 'moral terrorist' – and not only for his refusal to kill children. The Social Revolutionaries, in this interpretation, considered themselves the descendants of the *Narodnaia volia* ('People's will') revolutionaries and deliberately maintained their technique of making individuals approach their victims with hand-held bombs rather than, for example, fire a gun from a distance. In this sense they might be seen as early precursors of the modern suicide bomber, because the explosion often killed the assassin along with the victim. Another interpretation suggests that their willingness to risk their own lives to take the life of the representative of an evil regime was more evocative of the self-sacrifice of a Christian martyr.[25]

Walzer and Camus suggest that, unlike terrorists, who randomly kill innocent bystanders, the revolutionaries who assassinated members of the Romanov dynasty were following a certain moral code and their actions were morally justified. To a twenty-first-century observer living through the global war on terror, the distinction might seem anachronistic. In Russia's war to maintain control over the separatist republic of Chechnya, for example, desperate Chechen women have carried out suicide bombing attacks, in revenge for atrocities perpetrated against their loved ones. A careful study of the phenomenon concludes that 'the vast majority of suicide bombings have been directed at those whom the Chechen separatists consider combatants. The preponderance of these attacks have been directed at military installations and government compounds in and around Chechnya.' Nevertheless, the study refers to the perpetrators of these attacks as terrorists, even while implying that their cause is just.[26]

Walzer's analysis, published in the second half of the 1970s, seems in many ways a product of its time. The era of decolonization was coming to a close, many European states being forced to withdraw in the face of violent 'national liberation movements'. Walzer was particularly influenced by the failure of the United States to maintain control of Indochina after the French defeat at Dien Bien Phu and what he came to understand as the ultimate immorality of US military efforts to stay in Vietnam. The just cause of anti-colonialism and independence led observers to seek to find justice in the violent means that the national liberation forces employed. Moreover, not all observers drew even the sorts of distinctions that Walzer favored. Gillo Pontecorvo, the Italian director, in his 1966 film, *Battle of Algiers*, portrayed a press conference at which a captured leader of the Front de Libération Nationale was asked by an earnest young French journalist, in regard to the recent bomb attacks in the European quarter: 'Don't you find it rather cowardly to transport bombs in women's baskets and use them to kill innocent people?' He responded: 'And you, don't you find it much more cowardly to drop napalm bombs on defenseless villages and kill a thousand times more innocents? Give us your bombers, sir, and you can have our baskets.' In the midst of the US war in Vietnam, when anti-colonial sentiment was running high, one could imagine greater sympathy for terrorist methods than one observed in the wake of the 9/11 attacks. Many states, for example, endorsed the cause of the liberation of Vietnam from US control, whereas state support for al Qaeda seemed limited to some elements of Pakistani security forces, some members of the extended Saudi royal family, and what was left of the Taliban.

Many observers in the post-9/11 world seemed to find it difficult to justify political violence, even against the government and military officials of a repressive regime. The memory of armed resistance by partisan fighters to the German occupation of Europe during World War II – what the Nazi officials called terrorism – failed to inspire many parallels to contemporary terrorism. Few would have regretted the assassination of Adolf Hitler or, later, of Saddam Hussein, if the attempts had succeeded. But where to draw the line? In his historical examples, Walzer appeared to place autocratic Russia and democratic Britain in the same category when he admired adherence to the 'political code' by members of the SR and of the IRA, respectively. Even in the Russian case, however, one of the targets of a successful assassination was Aleksandr II, the reformist 'tsar liberator' who had freed the serfs. Was his murder justified to the same extent as the murder of one of his more repressive predecessors or successors would have been? Whose ethical evaluation should we accept? The assassin's?

One can understand the motivation behind Walzer's effort to find morally justified uses for non-state political violence. Yet today few states are likely to go along with it. One apparent exception is Switzerland. A provision of the Swiss Penal Code dealing with the financing of terrorism explicitly excludes from its scope acts of violence 'directed at the creation or restitution of conditions of democracy and the rule of law or at the exercise or protection of human rights'.[27] Such exceptions were common in international conventions on terrorism in the past, when violence conducted by Palestinians under Israeli occupation or by the military wing of the African National Congress in its struggle against apartheid received wide international sympathy. Now they are rare indeed.

Aside from the ethical considerations, there are pragmatic concerns associated with narrowing the definition of 'terrorist' so as to exclude political assassination. Excluding assassination from the definition risks endorsing the practice and reversing a centuries-long evolution toward stigmatizing state-sponsored assassinations of political leaders. Even in the case of Hitler, as Ward Thomas reports, British authorities rejected as 'unsportsmanlike' a 1938 proposal to assassinate him and did not make a deliberate effort to eliminate him until the final year of the war. That norm is now under some pressure, as Thomas discusses, but the benefits of doing away with it altogether, even in the interest of destroying evil tyrants, are still debatable.[28]

Whatever benefit violent revolutionaries might gain from obtaining moral sanction for their assassinations, they would lose it as states return in force to the assassination business. Assassination may be a classic weapon of the weak, but the strong can deploy it as well. In terms of our broader discussion of the factors that influence the strengthening or weakening of norms, Walzer's analysis leads to mixed conclusions. His suggestion that political assassination be excluded from the definition of terrorism has not caught on – at least for cases where individuals target state leaders. In that respect the norm against assassinations remains strong, as a state-centered (realist) approach would expect, given the threat they pose to states. Yet the norm appears to be weakening when it is a matter of states confronting non-state enemies. Several countries, including Israel, Russia, and the United States, have engaged in 'targeted killings' of suspected terrorists, justifying them as necessary for waging the war on terror. The next chapter considers whether such tactics are gaining the status of an accepted international norm.

International Conventions against Terrorism

To what extent have states' definitions of terrorism converged over the years? Is there yet a common normative understanding that could form the basis for collective action? By 2005, the United Nations, related agencies, and regional groupings of states had adopted some twenty conventions and protocols on various aspects of terrorism without agreeing on a consensus definition (see Table 2.2). A pre-9/11 treaty, the International Convention for the Suppression of Terrorist Bombings (1997), for example, defines the following terms in Article 1: State or government facility; infrastructure facility; explosive or other lethal device; military forces of a State; place of public use; and public transportation system. It does not define terrorism. The typical practice has been to smuggle in a definition in the course of condemning certain actions. Article 5 in the 1997 convention, for example, reads as follows:

> Each State Party shall adopt such measures as may be necessary, including, where appropriate, domestic legislation, to ensure that criminal acts within the scope of this Convention, in particular where they are intended or calculated to provoke a state of terror in the general public or in a group of persons or particular persons, are under no circumstances justifiable by considerations of a political, philosophical, ideological, racial, ethnic, religious or other similar nature and are punished by penalties consistent with their grave nature.

This particular formulation initially appeared in a UN General Assembly resolution in 1994. It was the first time that the prohibition of terrorist acts was not coupled with some mention of peoples' 'legitimate struggle for freedom and independence'.[29] Thus the provision serves to discredit the claim that one state's terrorist is another's freedom fighter. No act of terrorism is justified on any grounds. This passage has made its way into subsequent anti-terrorism resolutions and treaties, including the International Convention for the Suppression of Acts of Nuclear Terrorism of 2005 (Article 6).[30]

The International Convention for the Suppression of the Financing of Terrorism, adopted by the UN General Assembly in 1999, criminalizes the financial support of activities which are already banned by international convention, such as airplane hijacking and the abduction of diplomats. It then defines as terrorism 'any other act intended to cause death or serious bodily injury to a civilian, or to any other person not taking an active part in the hostilities in a situation of armed conflict, when the purpose of such act, by its nature or context, is to intimidate a population, or to compel a government or an international organization to do or to abstain from doing any act'.[31]

In September 2006, the United Nations General Assembly adopted a Global Counter-Terrorism Strategy. The document appears to define terrorism in its preamble when it states that 'acts, methods and practices of terrorism in all its forms and manifestations are activities aimed at the destruction of human rights, fundamental freedoms and democracy, threatening territorial integrity, security of States and destabilizing legitimately constituted Governments'. This formulation covers what terrorism *does* more than what it *is*. The mention of threats to territorial integrity risks associating the efforts of any secessionist movement with terrorism, even if those efforts are nonviolent. Moreover, terrorism is not the only activity that can lead to the destruction of human rights, freedom, and democracy. Some critics argue that many *anti*-terrorist measures have that effect. Is anti-terrorism therefore terrorism? The answer would seem to hinge on the meaning of the phrase 'aimed at'. Presumably democratic governments enacting anti-terror legislation and practices are not deliberately seeking to destroy democratic freedoms and human rights. That would free them from the charge of terrorism, but not from the charge of destroying freedoms and human rights. Sometimes their actions are so broad-reaching and potentially destructive that observers can hardly anticipate their consequences – as when the US legislative branch approved the Bush administration's law on electronic surveillance in August 2007, only to find that it gave the government far more sweeping powers to spy on Americans than the lawmakers had realized.[32] Legalizing harsh anti-terrorist measures such as torture can redound to the detriment of a state's security, leading to charges that the anti-terrorist cure is worse than the terrorist disease. In any event, equating terrorism with its consequences, when other actions can yield similar consequences, is no substitute for a definition.

Even without providing a definition of terrorism, the international conventions manage to address the controversial

Table 2.2. International conventions on terrorism

	Convention	Date of signing or adoption
United Nations Conventions	Convention on the Prevention and Punishment of Crimes against Internationally Protected Persons, including Diplomatic Agents	14 December 1973
	International Convention against the Taking of Hostages	17 December 1979
	International Convention for the Suppression of Terrorist Bombings	15 December 1997
	International Convention for the Suppression of the Financing of Terrorism	9 December 1999
	International Convention for the Suppression of Acts of Nuclear Terrorism	13 April 2005
Multilateral Conventions	Convention on Offences and Certain Other Acts Committed on Board Aircraft	14 September 1963
	Convention for the Suppression of Unlawful Seizure of Aircraft	16 December 1970
	Convention for the Suppression of Unlawful Acts against the Safety of Civil Aviation	23 September 1971
	Convention on the Physical Protection of Nuclear Material	3 March 1980
	Protocol on the Suppression of Unlawful Acts of Violence at Airports Serving International Civil Aviation, supplementary to the Convention for the Suppression of Unlawful Acts against the Safety of Civil Aviation	24 February 1988
	Convention for the Suppression of Unlawful Acts against the Safety of Maritime Navigation	10 March 1988
	Protocol for the Suppression of Unlawful Acts against the Safety of Fixed Platforms Located on the Continental Shelf	10 March 1988
	Convention on the Marking of Plastic Explosives for the Purpose of Detection	1 March 1991
Regional Conventions	Organization of American States Convention to Prevent and Punish Acts of Terrorism Taking the Form of Crimes against Persons and Related Extortion that are of International Significance	2 February 1971
	European Convention on the Suppression of Terrorism	27 January 1977
	South Asian Association for Regional Cooperation Regional Convention on Suppression of Terrorism	4 November 1987
	League of Arab States Convention on the Suppression of Terrorism	22 April 1998
	Treaty on Cooperation among States Members of the Commonwealth of Independent States in Combating Terrorism	4 June 1999
	Convention of the Organization of the Islamic Conference on Combating International Terrorism	1 July 1999
	Organization of African Unity Convention on the Prevention and Combating of Terrorism	14 July 1999

Source: http://untreatyun.org/English/Terrorism.asp.

issue of state terrorism. They essentially say that such actions are not the subject of these treaties, that they are already illegal under the laws of war. As the 1997 International Convention for the Suppression of Terrorist Bombings put it, 'the activities of military forces of States are governed by rules of international law outside the framework of this Convention'. It points out further that 'the exclusion of certain actions from the coverage of this Convention does not condone or make lawful otherwise unlawful acts, or preclude prosecution under other laws'.[33] The preamble to the Nuclear Terrorism Convention of 2005 includes identical language. The Plan of Action contained in the annex to the UN's Global Counter-Terrorism Strategy develops the point further, by vowing to recognize that 'international cooperation and any measures that we undertake to prevent and combat terrorism must comply with our obligations under international law, including the Charter of the United Nations and relevant international conventions and protocols, in particular human rights law, refugee law and international humanitarian law'.[34]

The insight into making definitional distinctions between war crimes carried out by states and terrorist acts committed by non-state actors was offered some years ago by A. P. Schmid: 'If the core of war crimes – deliberate attacks on civilians, hostage taking and the killing of prisoners – is extended to peacetime, we could simply define acts of terrorism as "peacetime equivalents of war crimes".'[35] The insight parallels in a way Michael Walzer's association of the 'war convention' with the 'political code' of violent revolutionaries. Whereas Walzer sought to identify the morally acceptable use of violence, Schmid focuses on criminalizing the political violence of individuals (terrorism) by associating it with the illegal violence of states (war crimes).

The main import of the formulations contained in all the recent UN conventions against terrorism is to point out that there is already a legal basis for holding states accountable for crimes against civilians, without there being a need to label those crimes 'terrorism'. International humanitarian law, including the Geneva Conventions, provides the appropriate venue.

There is a normative bargain implicit in UN terrorism conventions: States should not commit war crimes (and should punish the perpetrators when the crimes occur). Non-state actors should not engage in political violence – including the assassinations that Walzer's analysis would morally condone. But if we are not willing to accept narrowly targeted political violence of the sort that is consistent with Walzer's political code, we need to include a corollary to the UN's normative bargain – namely, that states must provide the possibility for peaceful challenges to the status quo and for democratic change.

In the United Nations, some clearly recognized a link between terrorism, counter-terrorism, and human rights. Mary Robinson, then UN High Commissioner for Human Rights, conveyed the point barely a half-year into the global war on terror: 'Impunity for those who have committed gross violations of human rights and grave breaches of humanitarian law', she argued, 'induces an atmosphere of fear and terror . . . encourages terrorist acts and undermines the international community's efforts to pursue justice under the law.' She maintained that 'ensuring that innocent people do not become the victims of counter-terrorism measures should always be an important component of any anti-terrorism strategy'.[36] The United Nations Global Counter-Terrorism Strategy contains similar language, suggesting an international consensus – at least at the rhetorical level.

Despite the rhetoric, there is a real danger that states will focus their attention on pursuing terrorists and will neglect to uphold their side of the human rights bargain. Some observers are not satisfied, for example, with the invocation of international humanitarian law in the terror conventions. Both the 1997 convention on terrorist bombings and the 2005 convention on nuclear terrorism exempt potentially criminal 'activities undertaken by military forces of a state in the exercise of their official duties', inasmuch as these are covered by other bodies of international law.[37] As one international jurist points out, 'although the intention to avoid interferences between conventional international criminal law and humanitarian law deserves support, it appears questionable whether the wholesale exemption of acts committed by members of armed forces from the scope of terrorism legislation is warranted. This may cause particularly reprehensible acts of "state terrorism" to escape criminal sanction when they are "governed by other rules of international law" that do not necessarily provide for individual punishment.'[38] Apart from national courts, the main vehicle for prosecuting individuals for war crimes and crimes against humanity is the International Criminal Court, an institution which the United States, among others, has refused to join.

Double Standards

One factor hindering attempts at cooperation around a consensus definition of terrorism has been state hypocrisy and the use of double standards. Even as a consensus emerges to leave state behavior out of international terrorism conventions, double standards continue to pose a barrier to effective enforcement. Given its high profile in the war on terror, the United States has come in for particular scrutiny. This section addresses three issues that highlight a problematic use of definitions of terrorism: the US government's refusal to extradite or prosecute an indicted international terrorist seeking safe haven on US territory; the US courts' unwillingness to apply terrorism statutes to armed groups conspiring to commit violence against immigrants, while they use those statutes to increase the prison sentences of environmental and animal rights activists; and the Bush administration's designation of another country's armed forces as a terrorist organization.

In May 2007 the US government refused to extradite Luis Posada Carriles, who had escaped from Venezuela in 1985 following indictment for his role in the 1976 bombing of a Cuban airliner. In addition to that attack, which killed seventy-three people, Posada was implicated in four other bombings, including that of the Guyanese Embassy in Trinidad. Posada was a longtime CIA agent, actively involved in illegal covert operations in Central America in the 1980s. His strong anti-communist views and his particular animus against the regime of Fidel Castro in Cuba apparently won Posada some sympathy in US government circles, even though his methods fitted most definitions of terrorist. Ironically, Posada evidently smuggled explosives onto the Cubana 455 flight by concealing them in a tube of toothpaste – a technique which caused particular alarm in the United States and Britain in August 2006, when evidence emerged of an alleged plot to bomb airlines by hiding explosive gels in hand luggage.[39]

Some domestic US cases of political violence also raise the question of double standards. In April 2007, for example, US federal authorities broke up a plot, by a group called the Alabama Free Militia, to attack some Mexican immigrants living in a small town north of Birmingham. According to the federal district attorney, police 'recovered 130 grenades, a grenade launcher, a machine gun, a short barreled shot-gun, two silencers, numerous other firearms, 2,500 rounds of ammunition, explosive components, approximately 70 improvised explosive devices (IED), and commercial fireworks'. The press release announcing the members' guilty pleas makes no mention of the presumed target of their planned attack, and none of the members was accused of conspiracy to commit terrorism. Instead they faced charges of conspiring to make firearms and other destructive devices.[40] As one commentator suggested, 'if these characters in Alabama were Arab Muslims, they would be on their way to some secret prison in Eastern Europe wearing diapers in a Learjet, ready to get waterboarded' – a reference to the 'extraordinary renditions' discussed in the next chapter.[41]

Given that the US courts let Luis Posada go free and limited prosecution of the Alabama anti-immigrant militia to firearms charges, the May 2007 verdict of an Oregon court may come as some surprise. Environmental and animal rights activists, after pleading guilty of 'conspiracy to damage or destroy private and government property', received a 'sentencing enhancement for terrorism'. It extended their prison terms and made them subject to incarceration in high-security facilities designed for violent terrorists. According to the judge's memorandum of opinion, the defendants were charged with conspiracy 'to commit a series of arson and other offenses on behalf of the Animal Liberation Front (ALF) and the Earth Liberation Front (ELF). The conspirators targeted federal government agencies and private parties they believed responsible for degradation of the environment, tree harvesting, and cruel treatment of animals.'[42] Although clearly engaged on the fringes of the environmental and animal rights movements, the defendants did not kill or harm any human beings, even if such a risk is presumably inherent in the crime of arson. Some observers argued that the court's decision set 'a dangerous precedent that could be exploited by the federal government to seek greater prison time for political activists engaged in acts of civil disobedience'.[43]

In August 2007, the Bush administration announced its consideration of a decision to declare Iran's Revolutionary Guard Corps a foreign terrorist organization. In October, the

US Senate passed a resolution supporting the measure, with Senator Hillary Clinton prominently advocating it. According to the *New York Times*, this 'would be the first time that the United States has added the armed forces of any sovereign government to its list of terrorist organizations'. *The Times* reported that 'the decision would have little impact on American military activities in Iraq, where coalition forces already pursue fighters, advisers and financiers who support antigovernment forces, according to a senior Defense Department official'.[44] Changing the status of Iran's Revolutionary Guards (estimated as the largest component of the national armed forces) to a terrorist organization would, however, have implications for a war with Iran. In the thinking of the Bush administration, the Guards would automatically become a military target, without need of a formal declaration of war or of the congressional authority normally mandated by the US Constitution. The 2006 edition of the *National Security Strategy of the United States* includes two passages that may be relevant. The first reiterates the US policy to attack 'the terrorists' rather than to seek to deter or defend against them: 'The United States can no longer simply rely on deterrence to keep the terrorists at bay or defensive measures to thwart them at the last moment. The fight must be taken to the enemy, to keep them on the run.' The second passage specifically refers to Iran: 'The United States and its allies in the War on Terror make no distinction between those who commit acts of terror and those who support and harbor them, because they are equally guilty of murder. Any government that chooses to be an ally of terror, such as Syria or Iran, has chosen to be an enemy of freedom, justice, and peace. The world must hold those regimes to account.'[45]

The Bush administration's position on Iran reflected another double standard when it began secretly to support armed groups to engage in terrorist attacks on Iranian soil. In a speech in January 2007, echoing the National Security Strategy, Bush accused Syria and Iran of 'allowing terrorists and insurgents to use their territory to move in and out of Iraq', where they would attack US forces. Investigative reporters Reese Erlich and Seymour Hersh have discovered that the United States is doing precisely the same thing. In its attempt to destabilize the Iranian regime, it has been providing funds to the Iranian affiliate of the Kurdistan Workers Party (known under its Kurdish initials, PKK) and to another group, called the Mujahadeen al-Halb, to engage in terrorism in Iran.[46] The US State Department has declared the PKK a terrorist organization, even if the group claims to fight for the rights of oppressed Iranian Kurds.

A final irony provides evidence of yet another double standard. In late November 2007, the *New York Times* reported, on the basis of information captured by the US military from computers found at a major Iraqi insurgent camp, that Iran was far from being the main source of instability in Iraq. Instead, the vast majority of foreign fighters in Iraq were coming from countries ostensibly friendly to the United States – Saudi Arabia and Libya, in particular. Neither the Bush administration nor Senator Clinton, however, proposed designating their regimes as state sponsors of terrorism.[47]

The decision to designate Iran's armed forces a terrorist organization would seem inconsistent with international terrorism conventions which exempt state military forces from their jurisdiction. Covert support for the PKK and for Mujahadeen al-Halb bolsters the cynical, traditional norm that one state's terrorist is another's freedom fighter. Thus both actions risk complicating international cooperation to combat terrorism. Moreover, suspicions were widespread that the actions were calculated to provide a casus belli for a US attack against Iran, especially if the Iranian government responded forcefully to the infiltration of terrorists into its territory. The

US would then justify a military operation against Iran, much as it did when it launched a war against Iraq in 2003 – as anticipatory self-defense against a major state which is a sponsor of international terrorism and an aspiring nuclear power. Chapter 4 takes up the topic of such preventive measures to fight terrorism and of the extent to which they can be seen to constitute an emerging norm of international behavior.

This chapter has described the difficulty states have encountered in trying to define terrorism in order to develop international conventions and cooperative measures to combat it. On the one hand, we observe an apparent weakening of the traditional norm that one state's terrorist is another's freedom fighter. International treaties gradually came to eliminate wording that would justify political violence for certain motives, such as self-determination, while stigmatizing it for others. On the other hand, the world's most powerful countries – the United States most prominently – continue to pursue double standards when it comes to deciding which individuals, groups, or states receive the designation 'terrorist' and which continue to get away with murder. The next chapter will reveal a similar double standard, at work in the matter of the status of suspected terrorists taken prisoners and those still at large. The prerogatives of states appear to dominate concerns for the human rights and the individual liberties of suspects whose complicity with terrorism may be far from certain.

CHAPTER THREE

Suspected Terrorists as Prisoners and Targets

One of the first ethical and legal controversies to arise in the wake of the 11 September attacks concerned detainees. As US forces engaged Taliban and al Qaeda fighters in Afghanistan, they began taking prisoners – some of whom could have information about future terrorist attacks. At the same time, US agents were offering bounties to members of the Northern Alliance – the armed forces that had fought against the Taliban for control of Afghanistan – for turning over al Qaeda and Taliban fighters. Many of the detainees ended up in a makeshift prison complex at Guantánamo Bay – a territory of the island of Cuba but under US control – as well as in secret prisons throughout the world.

Because the plot to attack the United States with civilian airliners involved al Qaeda networks in Europe and around the world, US officials also sought to capture suspects in various countries. These efforts sometimes included 'extraordinary rendition' – kidnapping individuals in one country and transporting them against their will to other countries where they would undergo interrogation, often under torture. Other alleged members of al Qaeda found safe haven in places such as Yemen, where the United States targeted them with missile strikes. The practice of long-range aerial attacks against individuals, without declaring or launching war, predates the Global War on Terror. In addition to the United States, other countries such as Israel and Russia have undertaken 'targeted killings' of this sort. The legal status of such attacks is controversial, with many observers claiming that they violate a long-standing taboo on political assassinations. Others maintain that the victims are 'enemy combatants' and therefore legal targets. From an ethical stand-point, some observers suggest that targeted killings are a morally superior way of dealing with threats because they limit the 'collateral damage' to innocent civilians – and one certainly preferable to all-out war.

The legal and ethical issues that these practices raise center around the status of terrorist suspects and their treatment. For those captured on the field of battle in Afghanistan, the question arose whether they would have the international legal status of prisoners of war, with rights guaranteed by the Geneva Conventions. For captives picked up elsewhere – say, on the streets of Milan – their legal status should have been more straightforward. No law permits armed agents, let alone foreign ones, to 'disappear' people for indefinite periods of time, without giving them access to lawyers or a way to contact family members. But if the suspects were designated as illegal 'enemy combatants', would that not make them legitimate targets in a war on terror? The treatment of the detainees, whether captured on or off a battlefield, involved well-documented physical and mental abuse that fits internation-ally recognized definitions of torture, thereby raising further ethical and legal concerns. The targeting of suspected terror-ists as enemy combatants raises somewhat different issues. These include: (1) the reliability of intelligence which can jus-tify, for example, having a cruise missile serve simultaneously as judge, jury, and executioner; and (2) the risks to innocent civilians, who can be harmed in the attacks.

War or Law Enforcement?

Early debates about the most appropriate way to deal with the terrorist threat that manifested itself in the 11 September attacks contrasted a *war paradigm* with one focusing on traditional *law enforcement*. The choice of paradigm bears directly on the question of how to treat terrorist suspects, whether in detention or at large. Before the 2001 attacks, the United States had dealt with Islamist terrorists through the criminal justice system. The Federal Bureau of Investigation, for example, identified Sheikh Omar Abdel Rahman and Ramzi Ahmed Yousef as key figures behind the 1993 bombing of the World Trade Center, and gathered enough evidence to convict them in a civilian court and to imprison them and all their accomplices. In order to capture them, US authorities used legal methods to infiltrate their organization, for instance informants wearing listening devices to record incriminating evidence. To convict them, US courts relied on domestic law, with all its protections in favor of the defendants.

For a brief moment, it appeared that US leaders might take a similar approach to al Qaeda's dramatic escalation of violence. In President Bush's first public remarks on 11 September, at the Emma Booker Elementary School in Sarasota, Florida, he referred to the attacks as a 'national tragedy' and vowed 'to conduct a full-scale investigation to hunt down and to find those folks who committed this act'. That same day, Attorney General John Ashcroft spoke of 'one of the greatest tragedies ever witnessed on our soil', and similarly promised 'to expend every effort and devote all the necessary resources to bring the people responsible for these acts, these crimes, to justice'.[1]

By the next day, however, the administration had changed the framing of the incident. Appearing for a photo opportunity with members of his national security team, President Bush announced that 'the deliberate and deadly attacks which were carried out yesterday against our country were more than acts of terror. They were acts of war.' He articulated two other themes that would henceforth characterize his portrayal of the event: The attacks were directed at 'not just our people, but all freedom-loving people', and the US response would entail 'a monumental struggle of good versus evil'.[2]

At this point the administration was unwilling to specify exactly with whom the United States found itself at war. Bush said 'a group of barbarians have declared war on the American people', and he named Osama bin Laden as 'a prime suspect'. Bin Laden at that point was still denying any role in the attacks, although five years earlier he himself had issued a 'Declaration of war against the Americans occupying the land of the two holy places'.[3] As the US government's 9/11 Commission Report points out, 'both President Clinton and President Bush chose not to seek a declaration of war on bin Ladin after he had declared war and had begun to wage it on us – a declaration they did not acknowledge publicly'.[4] In international law, only states have the authority to declare war anyhow, and only against other states. Despite its lack of formal grounding in law or practice, the struggle between al Qaeda and the United States came to be characterized by both sides as a war within days of the 9/11 attacks.

Returning from the site of the destruction of the twin towers, President Bush referred to the 'wreckage of New York City, the signs of the first battle of the war'. He vowed 'we will find those who did it; we will smoke them out of their holes; we will get them running and we'll bring them to justice'.[5] On more than one occasion when asked whether he sought to kill bin Laden, Bush invoked 'an old poster out west, as I recall, that said, "Wanted: Dead or Alive"'. He repeatedly referred to the terrorist 'evil-doers' – people 'who hate freedom', 'an enemy that likes to hide and burrow in' – and to his commitment to 'smoke them out'. 'This is a fight to say to the freedom-loving people of the world: we will not allow ourselves to be terrorized by somebody who thinks they can hit and hide in some cave somewhere.'[6]

We now know that the US Central Intelligence Agency became aware of al Qaeda's role in the 11 September plot within hours of the attacks. From the flight manifest of the plane that crashed into the Pentagon, agents recognized the names of two members of the organization. On 13 September, Cofer Black, the head of the CIA's Counter-Terrorist Center, had presented a plan to President Bush to hunt down al Qaeda in Afghanistan, using CIA operatives and US Army Special Forces which worked with armed Afghan groups opposed to the Taliban regime. According to George Tenet, the Director of Central Intelligence, the idea would be 'to take off the shackles' and allow the CIA to engage in activity from which it had been previously barred by US and international law. Black reportedly spoke of capturing al Qaeda leaders and putting 'their heads on sticks'. Around CIA headquarters and the White House, top officials spoke of bringing back the heads of Osama bin Laden and his top deputy Ayman al-Zawahiri 'in a box'. The CIA plan was evidently the inspiration for the preoccupation, revealed in President Bush's press conference, with smoking al Qaeda out of its caves and bringing in bin Laden 'dead or alive'.[7]

On 16 September, Vice President Richard Cheney alluded on national television to the belief of the Bush administration that it would have to resort to illegal and immoral methods in order to combat the terrorist threat. 'It's going to be vital', he said, 'to use any means at our disposal, basically, to achieve our objective', and this would include having to 'work through, sort of, the dark side'.[8] For US officials, the urgency of extracting information from suspected terrorists was paramount. In Washington, in the days following the September attacks, there was a palpable fear of further attempts. To the extent that ethical deliberations came into play, they adopted the character of ends justifying the means. Moreover, there seemed to be an assumption that physical and mental coercion represented the

most expedient means to achieve the ends of obtaining information that could save lives. Finally, there was an apparent
urgency on the part of US officials to be seen to *do something*.

A week after the attacks, the US Senate and House of
Representatives, in a joint resolution, authorized the president
to use force, essentially at his discretion, for a remarkably wide
range of contingencies:

> [T]he President is authorized to use all necessary and appro-
> priate force against those nations, organizations, or persons
> he determines planned, authorized, committed, or aided the
> terrorist attacks that occurred on September 11, 2001, or har-
> bored such organizations or persons, in order to prevent any
> future acts of international terrorism against the United
> States by such nations, organizations or persons.[9]

Out of 100 US Senators and 431 House members, only one –
Representative Barbara Lee of California – voted against granting the president such open-ended powers (and she received
death threats as a consequence). On that same day, 18
September 2001, President Bush signed a secret executive
order transferring between 800 and 900 million dollars to the
CIA, to begin implementing its counter-terror campaign. Two
days later, in a major speech, the president made explicit that
the campaign, now designated as a war, would be potentially
unlimited in time and space: 'Our "war on terror" begins with
al Qaeda, but it does not end there. It will not end until every
terrorist group of global reach has been found, stopped, and
defeated.'[10]

Much of the world sympathized with the civilian casualties
of the 11 September attacks. Support for the United States was
particularly strong in Europe, even among erstwhile critics of
US foreign policy. The headline of the French left-leaning
daily, *Le Monde*, epitomized the sentiment: 'We Are All
Americans.'[11] The first major US military response to the
attacks, the invasion of Afghanistan in October 2001, received

support from the UN Security Council and the North Atlantic Treaty Organization. By the spring of 2002, however, the European press began to call attention to ethical and legal lapses on the part of the US government in its war on terror. A triggering event was the report issued by Amnesty International in mid-April on conditions at the detention center established at the US military base on Guantánamo Bay.[12] The Bush administration's public campaign, initiated around the same time to justify a military invasion of Iraq, raised further concerns. Public attention to the treatment of prisoners reached a high point in April 2004, when Seymour Hersh of *The New Yorker* posted an article and photos (later published in the 10 May issue) exposing abuse of detainees at the Abu Ghraib prison in Iraq. In the United States, the *60 Minutes* television program brought the news to a wide audience, and it spread quickly throughout the world.

The main *empirical* questions that emerge from this course of developments include: How was the determination made of the legal status of the people captured in Afghanistan, Iraq, and elsewhere? How did the detainees become subject to physical and mental abuse constituting torture? In particular, was the process a top-down one, emanating from the highest levels of political leadership, or was it a bottom-up process, reflecting the confusion and frustration of troops on the ground dealing with a combination of terrorist and insurgent threats? The main *legal* questions concern what international law has to say about the status of the detainees and how the US courts, especially the Supreme Court, reacted to the Bush administration's decisions. Legal questions about torture are reasonably straightforward, as torture is illegal under international and US domestic law, but White House lawyers spent considerable time trying to define torture in very narrow terms. The main *ethical* question concerning torture is: can it be justified under any circumstances, even if it is illegal? Those who do not favor the current absolute ban on torture may want to consider whether the practice achieves the ends for which it is intended: do coercive interrogation techniques, for example, produce timely and accurate information? Absolutists in the torture debate consider the very questions themselves out of bounds, but the fact that most experts rate torture as a rather poor method of obtaining information should reinforce anti-torture sentiments.

Prisoners of Guantánamo

Starting in January 2002, US authorities transported over 500 prisoners to the Guantánamo base, never revealing the exact numbers or providing their names. The first public US commentary on the status accorded to the detainees came from then Secretary of Defense Donald Rumsfeld on 11 January. His remarks merit quoting at some length, both for what they reveal about his understanding of US legal obligations under the laws of war, and as an example of his unusual speaking style.

> I think that we're in the process of sorting through precisely the right way to handle them, and they will be handled in the right way. They will be handled not as prisoners of war, because they're not, but as unlawful combatants. The, as I understand it, technically unlawful combatants do not have any rights under the Geneva Convention. We have indicated that we do plan to, for the most part, treat them in a manner that is reasonably consistent with the Geneva Conventions, to the extent they are appropriate, and this is exactly what we have been doing.[13]

Rumsfeld's use of words such as 'precisely', 'right', and 'exactly' conveys confidence and determination to act correctly and in accordance with the law. He undermines that impression, however, with qualifying expressions such as 'for the most part', 'reasonably consistent', and 'to the extent they are appropriate'. Despite the verbal camouflage, the defense secretary's main conclusion is hard to miss: The detainees 'do not have any rights under the Geneva Convention'. The Bush administration declared its detainees illegal 'enemy combatants', not soldiers.

The drafters and signatories of the Geneva Conventions anticipated that not every person captured in the course of a war would enjoy the rights of a prisoner of war (POW). But there is a difference between meriting the specific, detailed rights of a POW and meriting no rights at all. The Third Geneva Convention of 1949 provides for the case of captives who may not enjoy the full rights of POWs. As Article 5 indicates, in case of doubt about their status, 'such persons shall enjoy the protection of the present Convention until such time as their status has been determined by a competent tribunal'. Along with most provisions of international humanitarian law, these have been incorporated into US military law and practice. In fact, the use of such tribunals, and their provenance in the Geneva Conventions, were so familiar to US military officers that the latter referred to them as 'Article 5 tribunals'. The edition of the US Army's Operational Law Handbook current at the time of Rumsfeld's press conference spells out the obligation in a paraphrase of the convention, referring to 'prisoner of war' as PW: 'When doubt exists as to whether captured enemy personnel warrant continued PW status, Art. 5 Tribunals must be convened.'[14] US armed forces made extensive use of Article 5 tribunals during the 1991 Gulf War, conducting 1,196 of them during Operation Desert Storm. The process resulted in 310 individuals receiving POW status. The others were determined to be civilians.[15]

Within a week, Secretary Rumsfeld recognized his error of interpretation and issued a clarification: 'Under the Geneva Convention, an unlawful combatant is entitled to humane treatment.' A White House policy statement followed in early

February 2002. It made the following points: the US will treat Guantánamo prisoners humanely and generally in a manner consistent with the Third Geneva Convention of 1949; the president has determined that the Geneva Convention applies to the Taliban detainees but not to the al Qaeda detainees; under the terms of the Geneva Convention, the Taliban detainees do not qualify as POWs; therefore, neither the Taliban nor al Qaeda detainees are entitled to POW status; even though the detainees are not entitled to POW privileges, they will be provided with many POW privileges as a matter of policy – but with some exceptions that the White House spelled out. Even though the Third Geneva Convention provides for the following privileges, the US administration did not intend to offer them to the Guantánamo prisoners: access to canteens to purchase food, soap, and tobacco; monthly advance of pay; ability to have and consult personal financial accounts; ability to receive scientific equipment, musical instruments, or sports outfits.

The White House press release was intended to defuse criticism about the handling of the detainees by insisting that they were treated humanely. What was the purpose of listing the privileges that the Guantánamo authorities would not provide to the prisoners? One may speculate that the administration was anticipating widespread understanding for its position that suspected terrorists (although it rarely used the adjective 'suspected') should not be allowed to have access to their bank accounts or to continue receiving their monthly salary, or to be permitted to pursue scientific, musical, and athletic activities. In a conventional war of limited duration between the professional armies of two states – the modal form of armed conflict assumed in the Geneva Conventions – such privileges might seem reasonable. In a war on terror, administration officials might argue, even the legalistic and holier-than-thou Europeans would understand the need to make exceptions.

> **Box 3.1 *Prisoner of war status according to the Geneva Conventions***
>
> *Should any doubt arise as to whether persons, having committed a belligerent act and having fallen into the hands of the enemy, belong to any of the categories enumerated in Article 4, such persons shall enjoy the protection of the present Convention until such time as their status has been determined by a competent tribunal.*
>
> • Article 5 of the Third Geneva Convention (1949)
>
> *Any person who has taken part in hostilities, who is not entitled to prisoner-of-war status and who does not benefit from more favourable treatment in accord with the Fourth [Geneva] Convention shall have the right at all times to the protection of Article 75 of this Protocol.*
>
> • Article 45(30) of the First 1977 Geneva Protocol
>
> Article 75 prohibits:
>
> • Violence to the life, health, or physical or mental well-being of persons, in particular
>   • Murder
>   • Torture of all kinds, whether physical or mental
>   • Corporal punishment
>   • Mutilation
> • Outrages upon personal dignity, in particular humiliating and degrading treatment, enforced prostitution and any form of indecent assault
> • Taking of hostages
> • Collective punishments
> • Threats to commit any of the foregoing acts
>
> *Source* The full texts are available on the website of the International Committee of the Red Cross, http://www.icrc.org/Web/Eng/siteeng0.nsf/htmlall/geneva conventions.

In fact, however, these were not the only exceptions the administration intended to make. In a memorandum prepared for the president a couple of weeks before the White House press release, Alberto Gonzales, then White House counsel, asserted that the 'new paradigm' of the war on terror 'renders obsolete Geneva's strict limitations on questioning of enemy prisoners and renders quaint some of its provisions'. When *Newsweek* magazine leaked the memo in May

2004, in the wake of the Abu Ghraib scandal, Gonzales came under criticism for his 'quaint' remark. If the White House policy had only referred to the denial of tobacco and musical instruments, as the press release implied, the criticism of Gonzales might have been considered excessive. In fact, however, the more significant way the White House intended to violate the Geneva Conventions came in the first part of Gonzales' quotation – in the 'strict limitations on questioning of enemy prisoners'. As Rosa Brooks suggested, 'lawyers for the Bush administration went from the legitimate conclusion that the Geneva Conventions cannot easily be applied to many modern conflicts, to the disingenuous and flawed conclusion that there were therefore no legal constraints at all on US interrogation practices'.[16] It is difficult to avoid the conclusion that the Bush administration's legal arguments which intended to deny POW status to all of the people captured in Afghanistan were driven primarily by the fact that the administration planned to use harsh and illegal methods to extract information from them about future terrorist attacks.

In retrospect, it appears that, with the January 2002 press release, the Bush administration sought to distract attention from these more serious violations of the law – the use of coercive physical and psychological methods to interrogate prisoners. Moreover, by responding, however disingenuously, to criticisms of the situation at Guantánamo, the White House managed to distract attention from even worse abuses taking place at the so-called Ghost Prisons – secret facilities hidden throughout the world where suspected 'high-value' prisoners were held.[17] Another serious problem with the administration's approach – one that would become more obvious as the years passed – is that it foresaw no end to the internment of the detainees. The Geneva Conventions provided for repatriation of prisoners of war at the end of hostilities. In the administration's view, the 'war on terror', in contrast to traditional wars, knew no territorial or temporal limits. If the Guantánamo detainees were not charged with crimes, they could languish in prison indefinitely.

The administration was slow in putting together the legal mechanism for trying the prisoners because it rejected both traditional courts martial and the civilian judicial system in favor of military commissions that provided few of the rights required for trials under the Geneva Conventions – a source of serious contention with the US Supreme Court, as we shall see. Nor was it apparent that many of the detainees had committed crimes for which there was enough evidence to try them. Donald Rumsfeld had described the detainees in early 2002 as 'the worst of the worst' and 'among the most dangerous, best-trained, vicious killers on the face of the earth'. But a CIA report from summer 2002 indicated that many of the detainees were noncombatants. Journalists tracked down witnesses in Afghanistan who maintained that many of the captives were 'aid workers who, as was the case for many detainees, had been captured and sold for bounty by tribal leaders, and who, after successive rounds of selling, had ended up in US custody'. When the Pentagon was obliged by the courts to make public its evidence on the detainees' status, the information contradicted the claims of the defense secretary and of President Bush. As Eric Umansky reported, 'most of the detainees hadn't been caught "on the battlefield" but rather mostly in Pakistan; fewer than half were accused of fighting against the US, and there was scant evidence to confirm that they were even combatants'. The Defense Department designated only 8 percent of the detainees at Guantánamo as 'al Qaeda fighters', and found that only 11 percent had been captured by coalition forces 'on the battlefield'. Several of the detainees were children, at least three of them between thirteen and fifteen years old. Yet, when President

Bush explained in a June 2006 press conference why it would be difficult to close down the Guantánamo facility, he repeated the claim that 'these people have been picked up off the battlefield, and they're very dangerous'.[18] The first part of the claim was clearly false, according to the government's own evidence. The second part could be true. After all, it would not be surprising if innocent people subjected to years of incarceration and abuse harbored a certain resentment and desire for vengeance. The lesson of British practices in Northern Ireland and of French practices in Algeria is, in the words of Alistair Horne, that prison 'is a marvelous recruiting and training centre'.[19]

The Bush administration's rejection of Article 5 tribunals to assess the status of detainees might seem surprising, given that the rules governing the tribunals totally favor the side controlling the prisoners. In traditional US practice, the tribunals themselves consist of US military officers with knowledge of the circumstances under which the detainees were captured, and their decisions are final – there is no right of appeal. That is why the United States used the tribunals so frequently and without controversy in the 1991 Gulf War.[20] The Bush administration's unwillingness to go through the normal legal channels, the ones reflected in the US Army's own regulations, seemed to indicate a particular animus towards international law and institutions. This is consistent with other actions undertaken as the administration first came into office – the 'unsigning' of the Rome Statute establishing the International Criminal Court, the rejection of the Kyoto Protocol on climate change, and the withdrawal from the Antiballistic Missile Treaty of 1972. It is in effect the international counterpart of the administration's apparent contempt for the laws of Congress and for the supervision of the courts, a product of the views on executive privilege and on the president's role as commander-in-chief which are widely held among Bush's advisers.

Commander-in-Chief above the Law

The White House public relations campaign to justify its treatment of detainees and the extensive legal preparation that
underpinned it would figure prominently in a top-down explanation for the crimes and abuses that came to light with
the revelations from Abu Ghraib. Lawyers in the Justice
Department and in the Office of the Counsel to the President
drafted memoranda intended to provide legal justification for
the Bush administration's treatment of detainees. Their interpretation of the US Constitution led them to favor executive
power at the expense of the legislature and the courts. Their
position on international law led them to argue that the United
States was obliged to adhere only to treaties that it had signed
and that had become part of federal law. That meant that, no
matter what norms of international humanitarian law or
human rights law would be considered customary by most
states, they would not apply. As John Yoo, an influential Justice
Department official, wrote in a draft memorandum to the
Pentagon's General Counsel in January 2002: 'Customary
international law has no binding legal effect on either the
President or the military because it is not federal law, as recognized by the Constitution.'[21] In August of that year, the
Assistant Attorney General Jay Bybee took an even stronger
position, claiming that 'any effort by Congress to regulate the
interrogation of battlefield combatants would violate the
Constitution's sole vesting of the Commander-in-Chief
authority in the President'. He argued that 'just as statutes that
order the President to conduct warfare in a certain manner or
for specific goals would be unconstitutional, so too are laws
that seek to prevent the President from gaining the intelligence he believes necessary to prevent attacks upon the United
States'. Bybee's report, largely the work of John Yoo, became
notorious as the so-called 'torture memo'. It defined torture so

> **Box 3.2** *US executive authority and the 'I'm not in favor of torture, but . . .' argument*
>
> **John Yoo** (Professor of Law, University of California, Berkeley, former Justice Department official):
>
> *I'm not saying I'm in favor of torture, but I am saying these are options to think about and these are arguments you would make in trying to figure out what interrogation techniques to use.*
>
> **Anne Marie Slaughter** (Professor of Law and Dean of the Woodrow Wilson School, Princeton University):
>
> *[I]f I hear you correctly, you are telling me that you would tell your client, the President of the United States, 'You may order pulling out somebody's fingernails. You may order having somebody's family member killed in front of them to extract information.' That is Constitutional. You are empowered to do that under the Constitution? Are you really saying that our Constitution allows a President to order that?*
>
> **John Yoo**: *Is there any provision that prevents him from doing that?*
>
> *Source* From the panel on 'Re-securing the homeland: Is the patriot act the right solution for homeland security?', Princeton University, 8 April 2005, pp. 14–15 of report; available at http://www.wws.princeton.edu/pcpia/2005/2005Report.pdf (downloaded 9 September 2007).

narrowly that hardly anything short of severe, prolonged pain specifically intended to pose the risk of death, organ failure, or permanent disability would qualify.[22] While arguing that the president had the authority to do anything he considered necessary in the war on terror, including breaking the law, the Justice Department lawyers sought to reinterpret the law, in case anyone disagreed. White House Counsel Gonzales had specifically asked Yoo and Bybee to determine whether any of the interrogation methods under consideration would subject US officials to prosecution by the International Criminal Court.

The Yoo-Bybee position on the relative powers of the executive and legislative branches in matters regarding war is an extreme one. A January 2007 report from the US Congressional Research Service provides a more mainstream view, certainly one more congenial to the legislature's point of view:

> The Constitution provides Congress with ample authority to legislate the treatment of battlefield detainees in the custody of the US military. The Constitution empowers Congress to make rules regarding capture on land or water, to define and punish violations of international law, and to make regulations to govern the armed forces. Congress also has the constitutional prerogative to declare war, a power it did not formally exercise with regard to the armed conflict in Afghanistan. By not declaring war, Congress has implicitly limited some presidential authorities.[23]

The view that the president's powers as commander-in-chief, vested in Article 2 of the US Constitution, put him, in effect, above the law – both domestic and international – was widely held within the Bush administration. It applied not only to the treatment of foreigners detained in the war on terror, but also to issues regarding the surveillance of American citizens. As the *New York Times* reported in August 2007, 'Bush administration officials have already signaled that, in their view, the president retains his constitutional authority to do whatever it takes to protect the country, regardless of any action Congress takes'. When legislators realized, for example, that they had signed a law permitting vastly greater spying ('wire-tapping') on electronic communications between citizens than they had intended, they sought unsuccessfully to get Bush administration officials even to agree to abide by the terms of the law as written. As the *New York Times* reported, 'senior Justice Department officials refused to commit the administration to adhering to the limits laid out in the new legislation and left open the possibility that the president could once again use what they have said in other instances is his constitutional authority to act outside the regulations set by Congress'.[24]

The Legal Status of Detainees

That the Bush administration was quick to neglect international legal standards for dealing with its captives does not
mean that their status under international law was obvious.
The status of the innocent people captured – students, children, aid workers – is not in doubt. They should never have
been arrested in the first place; once arrested, they should
have been freed after Article 5 tribunals established their inno-
cence. Regarding those who took up arms on behalf of al
Qaeda, however, there is controversy within the legal profession about some of the most basic aspects of the law. The al
Qaeda fighters do not seem to qualify as legal combatants or
soldiers under international law, yet it does not make sense to
consider them merely civilians either. As Brooks put it, 'the
boundary between civilians and combatants is one of the
oldest and most hallowed distinctions in the law of armed
conflict', yet al Qaeda seemed to fall somewhere in between.[25]
The phrase 'unlawful enemy combatant', which the Bush
administration applied to its detainees, does not appear in any
of the treaties of international humanitarian law, yet legal specialists have long discussed the category they variously call
unlawful or unprivileged combatants or belligerents. The first
point to understand is what is meant by the 'combatant's privilege'. The basic privilege of a combatant, employed by the
armed forces of a state, is the legal right to kill combatants of
another state with which his or her country is at war. Lawful
belligerents enjoy the related right to be treated as prisoners of
war, if they are captured, and not as common criminals who
could be put on trial and punished for their violent actions.
Civilians also enjoy rights under the law – specifically, the
right not to become deliberate targets of attack during the
fighting and to be treated humanely if they fall into the hands
of the enemy.

The laws of war evolved during the second half of the twentieth century to deal with combatants who were not members
of national armies but who did not seem to be common criminals and murderers either. These included armed members of
partisan resistance movements, as in Nazi-occupied Europe
during World War II, and fighters of the 'national liberation'
forces engaged in anti-colonial struggles. The principle of
according some rights to such fighters seemed based on the
inherent justice of their cause – the self-determination and
independence of their countries. Yet, in order to receive those
rights, the fighters had to meet certain criteria. According to
the Third Geneva Convention (1949) relevant to prisoners of
war, members of militias and 'organized resistance movements' would enjoy POW status if they met four conditions: (1)
they were 'commanded by a person responsible for his subordinates'; (2) they wore 'a fixed distinctive sign recognizable at a
distance'; (3) they carried their arms openly; and (4) they conducted 'their operations in accordance with the laws and cus-
toms of war'.[26] One purpose of requiring criteria that would
make such fighters resemble conventional armed forces
(chain of command, elements of a uniform, and so forth) was
to protect civilians. If the resistance forces were indistinguish-
able from civilians, opposing armies would not be able to
exercise discrimination in fighting them. The 1949 Geneva
Conventions and their subsequent elaboration in the 1977
Protocols did not fully resolve the issue of civilians at risk
during unconventional wars. After all, the main advantage of
guerrilla insurgents is their ability to blend into, and receive
support from, the civilian population – inevitably putting the
civilians in danger.

The al Qaeda fighters clearly failed to meet the criteria for
designation as lawful belligerents entitled to POW status.
Deliberately killing civilians is obviously not in conformity
with the laws of war. Nor was al Qaeda a disciplined military

force, wearing distinctive symbols and subject to a clear chain of command. Members of terrorist groups such as al Qaeda are guilty of murder if they kill even soldiers. If captured, they do not enjoy the rights of prisoners of war. Do they enjoy any protections? Here legal specialists disagree. Some would argue that, if detainees do not receive protection under the Third Convention on prisoners of war, they fall under the terms of the Fourth Convention, governing civilians – albeit civilians who illegally took up arms and can therefore be put on trial and punished for their crimes: 'A denial of POW status to captured enemy "combatants" does not make them legal pariahs. Such persons have to be considered as civilians.'[27] Others imply that the category of unprivileged belligerent falls outside the two conventions – the initial position articulated by Donald Rumsfeld. Michael Newton, for example, argued that 'persons who take part in hostilities without meeting the legal criteria as prisoners of war are neither protected civilians nor lawful combatants'. He suggested that Protocol I of 1977, which the United States did not sign, 'sustained the existing law of unlawful combatancy by specifying that civilians enjoy the protections embodied in the Protocol "unless and for such a time as they take a direct part in hostilities". The simplistic dualist position becomes unsustainable in light of this language because by definition a person who takes part in hostilities is not a civilian, but at the same time is not automatically entitled to prisoner of war status.' Nevertheless, Newton conceded that even a detainee not entitled to POW status receives the minimum protections of Article 75 (see Box 3.1), which prohibits murder, torture, corporal punishment, degrading and humiliating treatment, and even threats to do any of those things.[28]

Another controversial aspect of the policy of the Bush administration concerned the fact that the prisoners taken to Guantánamo included not only al Qaeda fighters, but also members of the Taliban, the nominal army of Afghanistan.

The administration made various arguments to bolster its decision not to accord Taliban fighters POW status, even though Afghanistan was a signatory to the Geneva Conventions. Administration lawyers suggested, for example, that Afghanistan was a 'failed state' – an expression not found in international treaties governing laws of warfare – and therefore neither US domestic law (the War Crimes Act of 1996) nor the Geneva Conventions applied. They argued further that the Taliban did not meet the conditions of Article 4(2) of the Third Convention regarding chain of command, insignia, open arms, and adherence to the laws of war.[29] Many legal scholars have argued, however, that these criteria do not need to be satisfied for a country's armed forces to qualify for POW status under Article 4(1), although presumably the four characteristics are part of what constitutes a legal army. The predominant legal understanding seems to be that if members of a national armed force fail to fulfill criteria such as wearing uniforms or obeying the laws of war, they can lose their POW status as *individuals* and can be prosecuted for war crimes – but they do not render their entire national army unlawful. If so, the US Army itself would be in trouble, as its special forces operated in Afghanistan disguised as civilians. As Michael Byers argued, 'if special forces – indeed, any soldiers – are captured operating out of uniform, they are not entitled to the protections owed to prisoners of war regardless of the country for which they fight'.[30]

Supreme Court Challenges and Administration Responses

As we have seen, the Bush administration denied POW status to Taliban and al Qaeda detainees without having used legally mandated Article 5 tribunals to determine that status. What did it intend to do with all those people? Most of the 500 or more prisoners held at Guantánamo were never charged with crimes, but eventually the administration identified fourteen individuals to put on trial. The most prominent figure was Salim Hamdan, a citizen of Yemen, who was accused of conspiracy to commit war crimes when he served as Osama bin Laden's driver and bodyguard and attended an al Qaeda camp in Afghanistan. The Geneva Conventions (Common Article 3) forbid 'the passing of sentences and the carrying out of executions without previous judgment by a regularly constituted court affording all the judicial guarantees which are recognized as indispensable by civilized peoples'.

The administration chose to ignore its international obligation and instead set up a special military commission (not to be confused with Article 5 tribunals) to try Hamdan. It was established by executive order in November 2001. As David Cole summarized:

> Its rules are draconian. They permit defendants to be tried and convicted on the basis of evidence that neither they nor their chosen civilian lawyers have any chance to see or rebut. They allow the use of hearsay evidence, which similarly deprives the defendant of an opportunity to cross-examine his accuser. They exclude information obtained by torture, but permit testimony coerced by any means short of torture. They deny the defendant the right to be present at all phases of his own trial. They empower the secretary of defense or his subordinate to intervene in the trial and decide central issues in the case instead of the presiding judge.[31]

Hamdan's lawyers challenged the legality of the military commissions as inconsistent with US obligations under the Geneva Conventions and won at the district court level. In June 2006, the US Supreme Court upheld the lower court's ruling.[32]

The Supreme Court's decision was particularly important for several reasons. First, it made clear that the Geneva

Conventions have the force of domestic law. The War Crimes Act, passed by Congress in 1996, makes it a felony, punishable in some instances by death, to violate Common Article 3 of the conventions. The article is found in all four Geneva Conventions of 1949 and is intended to cover 'armed conflict not of an international character', such as civil wars. Second, the court rejected the administration's contention that Common Article 3 does not apply to the al Qaeda detainees. The administration had argued that the war on terror was of an international character because the terrorists clearly had global reach and the US had fought al Qaeda in Afghanistan. The court chose to interpret 'international' literally, as referring to a traditional war between nation-states, and, because al Qaeda was a non-state actor, it could not fall into that category. Thus it was covered by Common Article 3. As far as the administration's detainee program was concerned, the article prohibited pretty much the same actions as Article 75 of the First Geneva Protocol of 1977, which most countries, but not the United States, have ratified: murder, mutilation, cruel treatment and torture, and 'outrages upon personal dignity, in particular humiliating and degrading treatment'. In other words, many of the techniques routinely applied to Guantánamo detainees and prisoners in secret prisons abroad – forcing them to go naked or wear women's underwear, attacking them with dogs, enforcing self-inflicted pain through stress positions, and so forth – were now called by their true names: war crimes. Legal experts pointed out that George Bush and other administration officials could be charged with violations of the War Crimes Act.[33]

The administration soon set to work to remedy the situation. It prepared legislation in the form of the Military Commissions Act, passed by Congress and signed into law in October 2006, in effect to legalize what the Supreme Court had declared unlawful. As its name implies, the act establishes the military commissions that the court had found illegal in Hamdan v.

Rumsfeld. Contrary to the 2004 Supreme Court decision in Rasul v. Bush, which granted Guantánamo prisoners habeas corpus rights to hear and contest the charges against them, the Military Commissions Act removes US courts' jurisdiction for anyone the government declares an 'enemy combatant' – and it does so retroactively. The act forbids anyone from appealing to the Geneva Conventions as a source of rights in any US court, thereby nullifying an important component of Hamdan v. Rumsfeld. By removing the Geneva protections, the administration allowed the military commissions to accept evidence by the means prohibited under Common Article 3: cruel, inhuman or degrading treatment or punishment, and 'outrages upon personal dignity, particularly humiliating or degrading treatment'. Finally, the act redefined torture, revising the federal criminal code concerning war crimes to make it echo the infamous 'torture memo' of August 2002. Evidence obtained by methods such as 'waterboarding', which induces fear of death by drowning, would now be admissible in court, along with secret and hearsay evidence.[34]

Why Torture?

The paper trail of memoranda concerning interrogation techniques and the deliberate rewriting of war-crimes legislation provide prima facie evidence of top-down initiative for the torture and abuse that became public knowledge with the Abu Ghraib scandal. Some observers suggest, on the contrary, that the initiative came from below. As US troops in Afghanistan began taking prisoners in October 2002, they believed that they had on their hands al Qaeda figures from whom they needed to extract information about future terrorist plots as quickly as possible. Yet, as Heather MacDonald argued, the 'interrogators in Afghanistan, and later in Cuba and Iraq, found virtually none of the terror detainees was giving up information – not in response to direct questioning, and not in response to army-approved psychological gambits for prisoners of war'. She offered a critique of what she called the 'torture narrative', that 'torturous interrogation methods, developed at Guantánamo Bay and Afghanistan in illegal disregard of Geneva protections, migrated to Abu Ghraib and were manifest in the abuse photos'. Instead, on the basis of her interviews with military personnel, she suggested an account that relieved high-level officials from responsibility for the crimes of Abu Ghraib. In response to the interrogators' inability to secure information about future terrorist attacks, 'debate erupted in detention centers across the globe about how to get detainees to talk. Were "stress techniques" – such as isolation or sleep deprivation to decrease a detainee's resistance to questioning – acceptable? Before the discussion concluded, however, the photos of prisoner abuse in Iraq's Abu Ghraib prison appeared.' [35]

The plausibility of the 'torture narrative', in MacDonald's view, required 'remaining ignorant of the actual interrogation techniques promulgated in the war on terror', which were 'light years from real torture and hedged around with bureaucratic safeguards'. MacDonald's account of the origins of Abu Ghraib focused on confusion at the ground level, combined with inadequate discipline and supervision from senior commanders.

> As the avalanche of prisoners taken in the street fighting overwhelmed the inadequate contingent of guards and officers at Abu Ghraib, order within the ranks broke down as thoroughly as order in the operation of the prison itself . . . No one knew who was in command. The guards' sadistic and sexualized treatment of prisoners was just an extension of the chaos they were already wallowing in with no restraint from above.

MacDonald's account comports well with the findings of a commission chaired by former official James Schlesinger to investigate the sources of the Abu Ghraib scandal. Schlesinger's report claimed to find 'no evidence of a policy of abuse promulgated by senior officials or military authorities', but rather a 'kind of Animal House on the night shift', a reference to the 1978 film about the drunken antics of members of a college fraternity.[36]

MacDonald's bottom-up account of responsibility for torture and abuse fares poorly in comparison with the overwhelming evidence compiled by journalists such as Mark Bowden, Mark Danner, Seymour Hersh, Jane Mayer, and Ron Susskind; historian Alfred McCoy, and human rights lawyer Jennifer Harbury – as well as with the many investigations conducted by the US armed forces themselves.[37] The story that clearly emerges is one of high-level initiative to loosen the legal constraints on interrogation, initially to gain information about future terrorist attacks, but later to pursue the war in Iraq as the US occupation came increasingly to meet resistance. John Yoo acknowledged that he drafted the 'torture memo' about which methods would be acceptable to inflict on captured al Qaeda leaders with one particular operative in mind: 'There was an urgency to decide so that valuable intelligence could be acquired from Abu Zubaydah, before further attacks could occur.'[38] Donald Rumsfeld penned hand-written comments on documents questioning the limits set on certain techniques, such as self-induced pain by prolonged forced standing ('I stand for 8–10 hours a day. Why is standing limited to 4 hours? D.R.').[39] George Bush took particular interest in 'how it's going on the ground'. He wanted to know 'which of our men really did the job' of capturing high-value suspects and how to get them to tell the truth: 'Do some of these harsh methods really work?'[40] That the president would insist on his prerogative to order torture in the face of apparent legal obstacles suggests a certain degree of high-level interest and complicity. The same holds for the vice-president's public advocacy of such methods as waterboarding. Responding to a talk-show host's question, he agreed that endorsing its use would be a 'no-brainer' for him.[41] In 2005, Porter Goss, the Director of Central

Intelligence, denied that any of the 'enhanced interrogation techniques' employed by the CIA constituted torture. These included waterboarding, which, in February 2008, the Bush administration acknowledged using against three specific al Qaeda suspects.[42] It has long been illegal for US soldiers to use this practice. From the war in the Philippines at the turn of the nineteenth century to the war in Vietnam, there are documented cases of US soldiers court-martialed and punished for waterboarding.[43]

The particular methods for inducing captives to reveal information were developed by CIA-funded academic researchers, carried out in places ranging from Vietnam to Honduras, adapted and implemented at Abu Ghraib and at secret prisons throughout the world.[44] Some of the more mundane methods, summarized by the *New York Times*, 'included slaps to the head; hours held naked in a frigid cell; days and nights without sleep while battered by thundering rock music; long periods manacled in stress positions; or the ultimate, waterboarding'.[45]

Why Bush administration officials were so eager to try these methods is not clear. There was considerable resistance within the professional military and among the seasoned investigators of the Federal Bureau of Investigation and some unease in the American Psychological Association because of the role that psychologists played in assisting interrogators with torture. Although the psychologists' association declined to ban its members from working in secret prisons where torture was used, the American Psychiatric Association reiterated its firm position that 'psychiatrists should not participate in, or otherwise assist or facilitate, the commission of torture of any person. Psychiatrists who become aware that torture has occurred, is occurring, or has been planned must report it promptly to a person or persons in a position to take corrective action.'[46] With the military and the FBI, much opposition was based on moral revulsion and reluctance to break the law. After all, torture is illegal throughout the world, and widely stigmatized. Another source of opposition was the belief that torture is a poor method for obtaining accurate information. Moreover, widespread torture and abuse of suspected terrorists in prisons tends to breed more terrorists. Finally, some interrogators were concerned that innocent people were being tortured. In 2003, US military intelligence officers told representatives of the International Committee of the Red Cross that between 70 and 90 percent of the people detained in Iraq 'had been arrested by mistake'. How many of them ended up being tortured in Abu Ghraib and elsewhere?[47]

The three types of opposition to torture match fairly well the debate about capital punishment. Absolutists believe that human beings have no right to decide on such life-or-death issues for fellow human beings and to violate their physical and mental integrity. Skeptics doubt that the practices produce what they promise: deterrence of crime by others in the case of the death penalty, prevention of terrorism in the case of torture. Everyone should understand that innocent people will inevitably become victims, through human error, of both capital punishment and torture.

The war on terror has already witnessed all three types of opposition to torture. The absolutist position is widely represented throughout the world. In October 2006, a 25-country poll posed a question about the morality of torture:

> Most countries have agreed to rules that prohibit torturing prisoners. Which position is closer to yours?
>
> 1 Terrorists pose such an extreme threat that governments should now be allowed to use some degree of torture if it may gain information that saves innocent lives.
> 2 Clear rules against torture should be maintained because any use of torture is immoral and will weaken international human rights standards against torture.

If we call the first position 'allow torture' and the second 'no torture', we can see from Table 3.1 that a majority of the world's population supports the absolutist view. The figures range from a high of 81 percent for Italy to a low of 23 percent for India, with the United States at 58 percent, just a point below the world average.

As for the skeptical view on torture's benefits, plenty of officials and former officials have come forward to express it and give examples. Within the CIA, the best a supporter of torture could muster, in an interview with Jane Mayer, was: 'All these methods produced useful information, but there was a lot that was bogus.' One former top agency official estimated that 'ninety percent of the information was unreliable'. Even one of the supposed success stories of CIA coercive interrogation, Khalid Sheik Mohammed, allegedly the main architect of the 11 September attacks, has made confessions that many insiders find doubtful – such as his boast that he personally executed the US journalist Daniel Pearl.[48] Mohammed had been subjected to 'a variety of tough interrogation tactics' which were 'used about 100 times over two weeks', according to former intelligence officials cited by the *New York Times* – to the point where even the CIA interrogators feared that 'the combined assault might have amounted to illegal torture'.[49] The case of Abu Zubaydah, about whom President Bush personally inquired, and on whose behalf John Yoo drafted his memo of torture methods, also raises questions about their effectiveness. In April 2002, Bush announced Zubaydah's capture and officials described him as 'chief of operations' for all of al Qaeda and 'number three' to bin Laden. He had been wounded in the attempt to escape being captured. 'He received the finest medical attention on the planet,' a CIA official told Ron Susskind. 'We got him in very good health, so we could start to torture him.' He was waterboarded, beaten, threatened with death, had his medication withheld and was 'bombarded

Table 3.1 International survey on torture

	Allow torture	No torture	Either/depends	No answer
Australia	22	75	2	1
Brazil	32	61	4	4
Canada	22	74	3	1
Chile	22	62	6	10
China	37	49	8	6
Egypt	25	65	6	3
France	19	75	4	2
Germany	21	71	6	1
India	32	23	28	17
Indonesia	40	51	4	4
Iraq	42	55	–	3
Israel	43	48	1	8
Italy	14	81	5	1
Kenya	38	53	3	6
Mexico	24	50	10	17
Nigeria	39	49	5	7
Philippines	40	56	2	3
Poland	27	62	5	7
S Korea	31	66	2	1
Russia	37	43	10	10
Spain	16	65	8	11
Turkey	24	62	7	7
Ukraine	29	54	11	7
UK	24	72	2	2
USA	36	58	4	3
average	29	59	6	6

Source BBC World Torture Poll, October 2006 http://www.worldpublicopinion.
org/pipa/pdf/oct06/BBC_Torture_Oct06_quaire.pdf

with deafening, continuous noise and harsh lights'. Susskind described what happened when Zubaydah 'broke':

> Under this duress, Zubaydah told them that shopping malls were targeted by al Qaeda. That information traveled the globe in an instant. Agents from the FBI, Secret Service, Customs, and various related agencies joined local police to surround malls. Zubaydah said banks – yes, banks – were a priority. FBI agents led officers in a race to surround and secure banks. And also supermarkets – al Qaeda was planning to blow up crowded supermarkets, several at one time. People would stop shopping. The nation's economy would be crippled. And the water systems – a target, too. Nuclear plants, naturally. And apartment buildings.[50]

Susskind's tone is obviously skeptical, and not only because his sources became dubious about what Zubaydah was telling them. Susskind reported that the best information that came out of the captive may have resulted from nonviolent methods of interrogation, such as discussions about the Qur'an and predestination by a knowledgeable CIA interrogator. In another case, Susskind described how the CIA peacefully infiltrated a bank in Pakistan that was laundering money for al Qaeda and managed to get the names and addresses of hundreds of operatives. Susskind's hunch about the limited usefulness of torture received corroboration in December 2006, when psychologists and other specialists drafted a 325-page initial report for the US Intelligence Science Board. It argued that the harsh interrogation techniques were 'outmoded, amateurish and unreliable', in the paraphrase of the journalists who broke the story and interviewed many of the report's authors.[51]

For those concerned that lifting the constraints on coercive interrogation would lead to the torture of innocents, the war on terror seems to have provided many examples. Maher Arar, a Canadian computer engineer born in Syria, was seized at Kennedy Airport in New York in September 2002, as he returned from holiday in Tunisia. A US government plane flew him to Syria, where he was held for ten months in a tiny cell and repeatedly beaten with a metal cable. Upon his release, the Canadian government exonerated him of any connection to terrorism and criticized Canadian officials who had provided false information to the United States. The US government, for its part, refused to acknowledge any wrongdoing or even to remove Arar from its watch list.[52] Khaled el-Masri, a resident of Germany, was abducted in December 2003 while in Macedonia and, by his account, was drugged, beaten, and flown to Afghanistan. There 'he was repeatedly beaten, kicked, photographed naked and forced to live in a cement cell with a filthy blanket for a bed'. He reported that the CIA released him five months later by dumping him in Albania. His was evidently a case of mistaken identity, as his surname was similar to that of someone on CIA's wanted list. One official admitted that the CIA was dealing with a number of such cases of 'erroneous renditions'.[53]

Harsh interrogations conducted as part of the wars in Afghanistan and Iraq have led to numerous crimes against civilians, including murder. A *New York Times* investigative report, based on army documents, described the sadistic brutalization of two Afghan detainees held by US forces. Autopsies revealed that they had died from 'blunt force injuries to the lower extremities'. The tissue in one young man's legs 'had basically been pulpified', according to the coroner. 'I've seen similar injuries in an individual run over by a bus.' In a version of the top-down explanation for the abuses, the *New York Times* reporter associated the crimes with high-level guidance, and misguidance, from the White House and the Pentagon, transmitted down the chain of command to local officers. He focused attention on, among others, Carolyn Wood, an army lieutenant (later promoted to captain) in her early thirties, who commanded the 525th Military Intelligence Brigade at Fort Bragg, North Carolina. Her unit of thirteen soldiers joined six Arabic-speaking reservists from the Utah National Guard to become part of Company A of the 519th Military Intelligence Battalion. Stationed at Bagram air force base in Afghanistan, the unit's soldiers were 'counterintelligence specialists with no background in interrogation. Only two of the soldiers had ever questioned actual prisoners.'

> Nor were the rules of engagement very clear. The platoon had the standard interrogations guide, Army Field Manual 34–52, and an order from the secretary of defense, Donald H. Rumsfeld, to treat prisoners 'humanely', and when possible, in accordance with the Geneva Conventions. But with President Bush's final determination in February 2002 that the Conventions did not apply to the conflict with Al Qaeda and that Taliban fighters would not be accorded the rights of prisoners of war, the interrogators believed they 'could deviate slightly from the rules', said one of the Utah reservists, Sgt. James A. Leahy. 'There was the Geneva Conventions for enemy prisoners of war, but nothing for terrorists,' Sergeant Leahy told Army investigators. And the detainees, senior intelligence officers said, were to be considered terrorists until proved otherwise.[54]

The presumption of guilty until proven innocent is a recipe for further crimes and a strong argument against the use of torture in interrogations. The consequence of the poor training and supervision was widespread abuse of the prisoners, including the two who were beaten to death under Captain Wood's watch in Afghanistan. Transferred to Iraq, she applied many of the same techniques to prisoners at Abu Ghraib.[55] But the ultimate responsibility rests at higher levels. Indeed, the Bush administration's decision to conflate al Qaeda terrorism with the war in Iraq insured that Iraqi insurgents, not to mention the hapless civilians caught up in counterinsurgency sweeps, would be at great risk of abuse. Moreover, the policy of offering bounties for turning in terrorists was rife with potential abuse.

If current US practice comes to shape the norms and laws that govern anti-terror operations, we should expect to see an eventual loosening of the stigma against torture. The logic might proceed along the lines that Henry Shue suggested, writing as he was well before the revelations of Abu Ghraib:

> We have no guarantee that a precedent of refraining from torture will be followed by others, but we can be sure that a precedent of engaging in torture will be followed. 'If the world's superpower, with all its high technology weapons, cannot defend itself without using torture, how can incomparably weaker and poorer groups like us manage without torturing captured fighters who might provide valuable life-saving information?' Torture seems to be the ultimate in efficiency, the shortcut to end all shortcuts. It is difficult enough to resist when you would be the exception if you gave in. When you would simply be following the leader, the precedent is irresistible.[56]

Countries that might be in a position to resist the new acceptance of torture, to refuse to 'follow the leader', might include those US allies whose views are accorded a degree of respect in the international public sphere.

That is why the complaint heard by a German court against Donald Rumsfeld and others, and mentioned in Chapter 1, was potentially so important. The US Center for Constitutional Rights pursued the case along with German colleagues, the International Federation for Human Rights, the Republican Attorneys' Association and others. It provided this summary:

> The complaint was filed under the Code of Crimes against International Law (CCIL), enacted by Germany in compliance with the Rome Statute creating the International Criminal Court in 2002, which Germany ratified. The CCIL provides for 'universal jurisdiction' for war crimes, crimes of genocide and crimes against humanity. It enables the German Federal Prosecutor to investigate and prosecute crimes constituting a violation of the CCIL, irrespective of the location of the defendant or plaintiff, the place where the crime was carried out, or the nationality of the persons involved.[57]

Box 3.3 *US officials named in criminal complaint for torture*

Former Secretary of Defense Donald Rumsfeld

Former CIA Director George Tenet

Undersecretary of Defense for Intelligence Dr. Stephen Cambone

Lieutenant General Ricardo Sanchez

Major General Walter Wojdakowski

Major General Geoffrey Miller

Colonel Thomas Pappas

Major General Barbara Fast

Colonel Marc Warren

Former Chief White House Counsel Alberto R. Gonzales

Former Assistant Attorney General Jay Bybee

Former Deputy Assistant Attorney General John Yoo

General Counsel of the Department of Defense William James Haynes, II

Vice President Chief Counsel David S. Addington

Source Center for Constitutional Rights, http://www.ccrny.org/v2/German
Case2006/germancase.asp

The complaint was filed on behalf of twelve Iraqis who suffered abuse and torture at Abu Ghraib prison and of a Saudi citizen detained at Guantánamo since January 2002. Extensive research into the provenance of the 'torture memos', high-level supervision of interrogation practices, and deliberate transfer of the methods from Guantánamo to Iraq yielded the names of thirteen officials, in addition to Rumsfeld, who were implicated in the crimes (see Box 3.3).

As Chapter 1 has indicated, the German prosecutor declined to continue the investigation and deferred to the US courts. But a US district court had already excused Rumsfeld from charges of torture, on the grounds that 'detaining and interrogating enemy aliens were the kinds of conduct the defendants were employed to perform'.[58] The German court's decision can probably not be said to have endorsed the new torture precedent, but it does seem to have supported the only-following-orders character of Rumsfeld's defense.

Targeted Killing and Assassination

Targeted killings entail some of the same ethical and legal issues as torture. Their primary intended victims, for example, are likely to be designated as enemy combatants. A key difference, of course, is that the goal of targeted killings is not to obtain information but to eliminate the victim. The preventive element is common to both practices and they are often understood to work in tandem: find out about attacks the terrorists are planning and kill them before they can carry them out.

The allure of targeted assassination is strengthened by the big 'what if' of 11 September. What if Osama bin Laden had been assassinated in the late 1990s? Would al Qaeda have carried out its deadly attacks against the United States? As a careful study by Ward Thomas has emphasized, such an act would have run contrary to 'a strong international norm that excludes assassination from the menu of foreign policy options, even when important interests are at stake'.[59] Writing on the eve of the 11 September attacks, when some US voices were already calling for the assassination of bin Laden, Thomas suggested that 'the temptation to strike directly at those most responsible for international mischief appears to be growing'.[60]

Officials in the administration of US President William Clinton felt that temptation in dealing with Osama bin Laden. Richard A. Clarke, the Clinton administration's counter-terrorism chief, described several attempted attacks in his testimony to the 9/11 Commission. By 1994, the CIA had identified bin Laden as a key 'terrorist financier', protected by the regime of Hasan Turabi in Sudan. Bin Laden later left for Afghanistan, when Sudan succumbed to the economic sanctions imposed for its unwillingness to turn him over. A US federal grand jury indicted bin Laden in 1998 and he responded with a *fatwa* which identified the United States and Israel as his main enemies. In August 1998, al Qaeda launched attacks against two US embassies in Kenya and Tanzania. The Clinton administration 'responded militarily with cruise missile attacks' on what Clarke described as al Qaeda facilities.[61]

Clarke's characterization depicts the cruise-missile attacks as both retaliation for previous terrorist attacks and attempts to disrupt the al Qaeda network – a preventive measure against further attacks. The legal status of such action was far from Clarke's mind as he presented his testimony. A key goal of the 9/11 Commission was to understand how US national security authorities had failed to prevent the September attacks. Had they underestimated the threat posed by al Qaeda? Clarke's objective was to suggest that the Clinton administration had, in fact, tried to damage the organization. No one on the Commission asked if the acts were legal. If the United States had succeeded in destroying al Qaeda and in killing bin Laden in 1998, perhaps some legal specialists and some countries would have accused it of breaking the law. If they had known what al Qaeda was capable of – mass murder of thousands of civilians – would that have affected their legal or moral judgment?

Previous historical cases suggest that states use legal arguments instrumentally, in the service of their political goals, even when such arguments would seem to contradict common-sense moral judgments and to delay potentially beneficial changes in international practice. Yet, if enough states support those changes, they can become accepted and attain legal status. In this regard, Michael Byers, a leading authority on customary international law, cited the example of Israel's Entebbe rescue operation. In June 1967, pro-Palestinian hijackers seized an Air France plane and forced it to land in Entebbe, Uganda. They issued an ultimatum for the release of fifty-three accused terrorists, else the Israeli passengers held hostage would be killed. When the Ugandan dictator Idi Amin made no effort to secure their release, Israel took matters into its own hands and freed the hostages by staging a daring commando raid. The rescue saved the lives of all but three of the passengers. Several Ugandan soldiers died, but only one Israeli commando was killed – Yonatan Netanyahu, whose brother Binyamin later became a prominent politician. Israel's friends cheered the successful rescue mission, with Britain and the United States seeking a UN Security Council resolution to condemn the hijacking, and, implicitly, to endorse Israel's action. They were unable to attract enough votes to pass the resolution, as seven states were unwilling even to participate in the discussion. A second draft resolution, offered by rotating Security Council members, including Libya, sought to condemn Israel for the violation of Uganda's territorial integrity and sovereignty. It was never put to a vote. Despite this ambiguous outcome, Byers argued that the mixed reception of Israel's action signaled a tacit acceptance of its argument: 'Today, the Entebbe incident is regarded as having decisively contributed to a limited extension of the right of self-defence in international affairs to include the protection of nationals abroad.'[62]

Could a similar change in attitude lead to widespread acceptance of targeted attacks against individuals? There is a difference, of course, between using military force to rescue hostages held by terrorists and the two goals which have been at the center of US anti-terror policy since before the emergence of al Qaeda. US policy has focused on: (1) retaliation for terrorist acts; and (2) preemptive or preventive use of force to disrupt terrorist networks, often by killing individual members. Whether the practices become commonly accepted depends in part on whether they are seen to be effective as well as legally and morally sound.

Consider another historical example, this time involving the United States. In 1986, a bomb exploded in a discothèque in Berlin frequented by US soldiers and killed two of them, along with a Turkish woman. US intelligence linked the attack to the Libyan regime of Muammar Qadhafi. Then President Ronald Reagan ordered a retaliatory strike against Tripoli. As the 9/11 Commission Report recalled, 'the operation was not cost free: the United States lost two planes'. It failed to mention the deaths of 15 civilians, including a baby girl, claimed to be Colonel Qadhafi's adopted daughter. According to the 9/11 Commission, the operation 'was seen at the time as a success', imparting the lesson that 'terrorism could be stopped by the use of US air power that inflicted pain on the authors or sponsors of terrorist acts'. This was a dubious conclusion to draw, however, given that Qadhafi responded to the US air attack with several further acts of terrorism, which culminated in the bombing of Pan Am Flight 103 over Lockerbie, Scotland in December 1988. Nevertheless, as the report continued, the lesson that retaliatory air power could stop terrorism 'was applied, using Tomahawk cruise missiles, early in the Clinton administration'.[63]

The Clinton administration's first use of retaliatory force came in 1993, not in response to a terrorist attack but to intelligence information about a planned attack: a plot to assassinate former President George H. W. Bush on his visit to Kuwait to receive thanks for his role in overseeing the 1991 war, which ended the Iraqi occupation of that country. The Pentagon prepared a list of twelve targets, but the White House pared it down to one. On 27 June 1993, twenty-three missiles were launched against the headquarters of the Iraqi intelligence services in Baghdad, destroying the complex and killing apparently only one civilian.[64]

Some US observers, far from criticizing the legality of Clinton's retaliatory strike, excoriated him for not doing more. As William Safire wrote,

He could have directed US bombers located in Turkey to dev-
astate Saddam's Republican Guard, source of his dictatorial
power, now lined up in tanks and armored vehicles threatening the Kurds and Shiites. He could have turned out the lights
in Iraq and set back its oil-production capacity, which – combined with a reduction of his Republican Guard and the
arming of the anti-Saddam forces in the North – could endanger the regime itself. Not one of these reactions required UN
approval; the murder plot was against a US President. But
Mr. Clinton chose the course that Stewart Alsop used to label
'phony-tough': He threw a score of missiles at a building after
its officials had left for the day . . . [W]hen one head of state
tries to murder another, that is an act of war. If clear evidence
had shown that Fidel Castro ordered the killing of President
Kennedy, President Johnson would surely have used military
force to depose the regime in Havana.[65]

Safire here unintentionally raised the issue of double standards, an occupational hazard of major powers. Any link
between Fidel Castro and the assassination of John F. Kennedy
has yet to be conclusively demonstrated. But it is well known
that the Kennedy administration tried on many occasions to
assassinate Castro and sponsored the unsuccessful Bay of Pigs
invasion of Cuba in April 1961. Would Cuba have been justified, then, in launching an invasion or in retaliating against the
Kennedy estate in Palm Beach, Florida? In fact, it was the CIA's
overzealous pursuit of assassination and other 'dirty tricks'
that led Senator Frank Church to conduct investigations in the
mid-1970s which prompted President Gerald Ford to issue an
executive order banning political assassinations.[66]

International political assassinations are still widely recognized as illegal, although the targeting of political leaders who
serve as military commanders during war is generally considered lawful. As Gary Solis pointed out, Saddam Hussein
during wartime 'was a combatant and lawful target, since he
customarily wore a military uniform and went armed, often in

the vanguard of Iraqi military units'. The president of the United States, denominated by the US Constitution as commander-in-chief of the armed forces, is also 'a lawful target for an opposing state's combatants', according to Solis. 'He is the person whom the chairman of the Joint Chiefs of Staff advises', and 'the final authority for the strategic disposition of US armed forces'.[67] Other political leaders, such as prime ministers and constitutional monarchs, typically do not fulfill the criteria for wartime command, and would consequently not be considered legal targets.

There was some consideration given to assassinating Saddam Hussein as an alternative to launching the preventive war discussed in the next chapter. The opening hours of that war, on 19 March 2003, did in fact witness an attempt at what is known in the jargon as 'decapitation' – unsuccessful, as it turned out. The US Navy launched some forty-five Tomahawk land-attack missiles, intended to kill the Iraqi dictator. Each missile 'carried a 1,000-pound warhead, guaranteed to pulverize every structure in the vicinity'. The CIA 'was 99.9 percent sure it had located Saddam and both of his sons', but in retrospect it became clear that Saddam Hussein had been nowhere near that site, on the outskirts of Baghdad.[68] Many civilians, however, had arrived in the area, having fled the central city, expecting that Saddam's palaces there would be the main targets. According to the research of Human Rights Watch, the United States targeted, all in all, fifty top Iraqi leaders with such decapitation strikes, and hit not one of them. The toll of 'collateral damage' in civilian death and destruction was, however, quite high. When a Human Rights Watch interviewer asked how carefully the US Air Force reviewed strikes in Iraq for collateral damage, a senior US Central Command official responded, 'with excruciating pain' – an unfortunate choice of words, under the circumstances.[69] If targeted assassination in lieu of war promises to spare civilian lives, targeted decapitation strikes in the course of war do no such thing – at least if the 2003 Iraq War is an example. In this case, the weapons were disproportionately large and the intelligence was disproportionately inaccurate.

The main states involved in the practice of targeted killing have been Israel and the United States. In its decade-long war against the secessionist Republic of Chechnya, Russia managed to kill two successive leaders – Djokhar Dudaev and Aslan Maskhadov – in the case of Dudaev, by using guided missiles to home in on his satellite phone signal. Although popular sources (the Wikipedia website, for example) might deem these killings assassinations, both Dudaev and Maskhadov were military generals commanding an armed resistance, and therefore legitimate targets. (Russian authorities are also accused of having killed journalists and political opponents of the war.) The status of the targets of US and Israeli attacks is more ambiguous, not least because of the ambiguous status of each country's 'war' on 'terror'.

The most straightforward case for killing unlawful combatants can be made when they are engaged in combat and pose a threat to a state's armed forces, as in the example of al Qaeda facing the US Army on the battlefields of Afghanistan. Most of the other cases are far more controversial. In September 2002, for example, an Israeli helicopter gunship fired two 100-pound Hellfire anti-tank missiles at the car of Muhammad Deif, head of the military wing of Hamas, who was considered responsible for organizing suicide bombings, kidnappings, and murders. He survived the attack but his two body-guards were killed and forty-three passers-by, including fifteen schoolchildren, were wounded. Two months earlier, Israel had killed Deif's predecessor, Sheikh Salah Shehada, by dropping a one-ton bomb that killed sixteen other people as well.[70]

These two cases raise a number of issues that allow us to apply the same legal and ethical frameworks we have employed in dealing with other questions related to targeted killings. One issue that has not been a major focus in this book, but that is relevant, is whether the various elements of the 'war on terror' constitute armed conflict of an international or non-international character, as defined in international humanitarian law. This question is covered well elsewhere.[71] Both Israel and the United States have accepted that the laws of war govern some of their behavior in their conflicts with terrorists.

What we consider here is what the law has to say about unlawful combatants and about when they can be targeted for killing. Most legal scholars focus on Article 51(3) of the First Geneva Protocol (1977) to ascertain when civilians lose their protected status: 'Civilians shall enjoy the protection afforded by this Section, unless and for such time as they take a direct part in hostilities.' Typical of legal analysis of an issue where the body of law is relatively scant, this passage comes in for much parsing in every component. What does it mean to take 'a direct part' in hostilities, for example? Does the passage 'for such time' indicate that as soon as unlawful belligerents cease fighting they regain the protections from attack to which civilians are entitled? The more permissive a state's rule for targeting killings is, the more likely it is that these components of Article 51(3) will receive the loosest interpretation. Kathleen Cavanaugh pointed out, for example, that 'Israel has provided an elastic interpretation of taking "direct part", arguing that this includes execution, *planning or dispatching*' (her emphasis), whereas more traditional interpretations are more limited. She favored the more limited definition also regarding time: 'Civilians who engage in hostilities are lawful targets for the period, and *only the period*, that they participate directly in hostilities' (her emphasis). Otherwise, she argued, civilians who engage in war crimes by becoming unlawful belligerents are denied their rights to a trial. This was precisely the principle that the US Supreme Court sought to uphold in Hamdan v. Rumsfeld when it cited the provision of Common Article 3, regarding trial by a 'regularly constituted court affording all the judicial guarantees which are recognized as indispensable by civilized peoples'. Cavanaugh pointed out that previous Supreme Court decisions going back to *Ex parte Quirin* of 1942 maintained that guerrilla fighters and even spies must be put on trial before they are punished for their crimes, so suspected terrorists presumably should receive the same treatment.[72]

Other specialists have found such interpretations too generous. Kenneth Watkin wrote, for example, of the 'danger that the term "for such time" will lead to an interpretation that civilians are only combatants while they carry a weapon and revert to civilian status once they throw down a rifle or return home from a day in the trenches'. He rejected this 'revolving door' of protection for certain civilians. 'Taken to its extreme,' he argued, 'such a narrow interpretation appears not only to protect civilians who might be confused with participants in hostilities, but also indirectly to provide cover for the actual participants themselves, despite their prior and possible future hostile acts.'[73] Clearly, the advocates of targeted killings in Israel, the United States, and elsewhere find themselves in agreement with the looser understandings of 'to take part in hostilities' and 'for such time'.

Even if there were agreement that a given civilian/unlawful belligerent were a legitimate target, there is still room for disagreement about the means for killing him or her. The contrast between the two attacks on the Hamas leaders, for example, illustrates the tension between two principles of just war theory – reasonable hope and proportionality. The Israeli government came under criticism at home and abroad for dropping the one-ton bomb on the densely populated Daraj neighborhood in its successful attempt to kill Shehada, because the attack killed his daughter and fourteen others, ten of them children. Was the military benefit of killing Shehada proportionate with the harm done to fifteen innocents? In the case of the attempt against Deif, the Israeli authorities came under criticism (mainly at home) for using *insufficient* force.[74] If there was no reasonable hope of killing Deif with a 100-pound bomb, it would seem unethical to put the passers-by at risk.

The United States has faced similar issues regarding proportionality in the targeted killings it has carried out in the war on terror. An attack against the town of Damadola in Pakistan in January 2006 reportedly killed at least four al-Qaeda members, but missed its intended target, Ayman al-Zawahiri, who was not present. Eighteen civilians – including five children – were supposed to have died in the strike. In response to the attack, Gary Solis raised precisely the question of proportionality, by asking: 'How many lives is the No. 2 of al-Qaeda worth?' Senator John McCain's reaction, by contrast, suggested a lack of understanding of the concept: 'It's terrible when innocent people are killed; we regret that,' he told CBS television. 'But we have to do what we think is necessary to take out al-Qaeda, particularly the top operatives. This guy has been more visible than Osama bin Laden lately.'[75]

The attack against Pakistan, and the ones against suspected al Qaeda militants in Somalia a year later, pose a further set of considerations, of a more pragmatic sort. Like torture, targeting killings can have a counterproductive effect – they lead to more terrorism rather than less. In the Israeli–Palestinian conflict, each side insists that the other's violence begets further violence, and both sides are probably right. Given how unpopular the United States is throughout the world, but especially in places like Pakistan and Somalia, US leaders might want to consider whether their actions aimed at preventing terrorism could serve as a recruiting call for new terrorists. Apart from the legality and morality of targeted killings, their effectiveness may influence the issue of whether they come to be considered acceptable state practice.

In Iraq in 2007, the US Defense Department's Asymmetrical Warfare Group trained Army Rangers to place fake weapons and bomb materials for unarmed Iraqis to pick up, at which point the snipers would kill them. The classified 'baiting program' came to light when the Army brought the snipers before a court martial and accused them of murdering Iraqi civilians. According to the *New York Times*, the soldiers exposed the program in an effort to use the 'we-were-only-following-orders' defense, generally discredited since the Nazis tried it at Nuremberg: 'Through their lawyers and in court documents, the soldiers say the killings were legal and authorized by their superiors.' Nevertheless, the soldiers appear to have had some doubts about the legality of their actions. In addition to murder, they were accused of having planted incriminating evidence on the corpses – in particular, detonation wires and other 'drop weapons', as they are known. A spokesperson claimed that 'the Army did not publicly discuss specific methods for "targeting enemy combatants", and that no classified program authorized the use of 'drop weapons' to make a killing appear justified'. Army officers involved in the evidentiary hearings in Baghdad did not, however, 'dispute the existence or use of a baiting program'.[76] This incident suggests a profound confusion within the US Army itself about the meaning of 'enemy combatant'. For the army prosecutors in the court martial, the snipers' victims were civilians and the Rangers were committing murder. For the army spokesperson, the victims were 'enemy combatants' and the Rangers were shooting legitimate targets.

The law governing treatment of suspected terrorists is clearly in flux. There is little agreement about how such people should be handled when taken prisoner, or whether they can be targeted under any conditions except when they are taking direct part in hostilities in the most literal sense. By subjecting its detainees to torture, the United States violated unambiguous legal strictures and fundamental principles of morality. The US Army itself challenged the legality of its own program of baiting and killing potential bomb makers. Under the circumstances, one might doubt that the US practices of torturing detainees and killing suspected 'enemy combatants' could come to constitute a new norm of international behavior. On the other hand, there has been very little public opposition to such practices in the United States. In the autumn of 2007, some US Senators expressed concern that the Bush administration's nominee for attorney general, Michael Mukasey, refused even to acknowledge waterboarding as a form of torture, let alone express a principled opposition to the practice. Nevertheless, the Senate approved his nomination and the issue of torture disappeared again from the public debate. Outside the United States, we observe two contradictory tendencies. In some countries criticism of torture has persisted, which suggests resistance to weakening the norm against the practice. In other countries, however, torture has made a come-back, following the logic of precedent that Henry Shue articulated. There is good evidence, for example, that in countries such as Morocco, which had seen an eradication of routine torture in the course of recent political liberalization, the practice has returned – thanks in part to the United States' rendition of suspected terrorists to Morocco for interrogation.[77] Given the ambiguous US and international attitudes towards torture and 'disappearances' of the extraordinary rendition sort, we cannot with any confidence assert that such practices will retain the stigma that human rights activists worked so hard to attach to them.

The US endorsement of preventive military action in its war on terror has also met with mixed responses at home and abroad. In the wake of the largely negative reaction to the first US effort to put theory into practice – the invasion of Iraq in March 2003 – international attitudes towards preventive war were more sympathetic than one might have expected. The next chapter poses the question whether an international norm in support of the practice began to emerge in the early twenty-first century, despite widespread suspicion of US intentions.

CHAPTER FOUR

Preventive War: An Emerging Norm?

In response to the challenge of transnational terrorism, the United States has engaged in practices that raise questions about its compliance with the laws of war and other international obligations. It has claimed the right, and exercised it in Iraq, to invade countries that it suspects of harboring terrorists and/or developing weapons of mass destruction. It has justified this practice using the terminology of legally sanctioned behavior such as anticipatory self-defense and preemption, yet most observers consider the invasion of Iraq an instance of preventive war – whose legal status is more dubious. This chapter starts by distinguishing between the rationale for the post-9/11 invasion of Afghanistan and the 2003 Iraq War. It next explores the logic underlying the Bush administration's attack on Iraq, with particular focus on the so-called 'one percent doctrine' associated with Vice President Richard Cheney. It then reviews the evidence that suggests a greater international acceptance of the preventive motive for military action, despite the widespread global opposition to the invasion of Iraq itself.

The Afghanistan War as Self-Defense

In the wake of the 11 September 2001 attacks, the United States launched a war against Afghanistan. The Taliban regime running the country had offered safe haven to Osama bin Laden and to members of his al Qaeda network, and had refused, both before and after the attacks, to turn them over to the United States for prosecution. Bin Laden had been living in Afghanistan and running terrorist training camps there since 1996. At the last moment, the Taliban leadership offered to surrender bin Laden to a neutral third party, but the US government did not find the offer credible or acceptable. Moreover, as early as 1999 the United Nations Security Council had issued a resolution, invoking Chapter VII of the UN Charter (regarding threats to international peace and security), which required the Taliban to extradite bin Laden to the United States – a US court had indicted him the year before for attacks against US embassies in Africa – or to a third country that would send him to the United States.

Because of the Taliban's recalcitrance and the widespread revulsion against the 11 September attacks, the US-led war in Afghanistan, which initially involved air attacks and the introduction of Special Forces to track down al Qaeda figures, received broad international endorsement as an act of self-defense. Members of the North Atlantic Treaty Organization, for the first time in its history, invoked Article 5 of the NATO Charter, stipulating that an attack against one would be considered an attack against all, and offered military support to the United States. The Bush administration was not much interested in NATO support, but did allow the British to contribute to the war effort. The United Nations Security Council issued two resolutions, 1368 and 1373, on 12 and 28 September 2001 respectively, which seemed to endorse the US use of force. Both resolutions invoked 'the inherent right of individual or collective self-defense as recognized by the Charter of the United Nations'. The earlier resolution calls 'on all States to work together urgently to bring to justice the perpetrators, organizers and sponsors of these terrorist attacks and stresses that those responsible for aiding, supporting or harboring the perpetrators, organizers and sponsors of these acts will be held accountable'. The latter reaffirms 'the need to combat by all means, in accordance with the Charter of the United Nations, threats to international peace and security caused by terrorist acts'.[1] The explicit reference to an inherent right of self-defense, the invocation of the UN Charter, and the expression 'combat by all means' gave the green light to the US invasion.

Thoughtful critics have disagreed with the Bush administration that the resort to war was the only available recourse for apprehending bin Laden and for forestalling further terrorist attacks.[2] That the US invasion of Afghanistan failed to capture bin Laden and that terrorist attacks continued – in Bali, Madrid, and London, for example – does not necessarily validate that criticism. But these events do suggest that war provided no panacea for the problem of international terrorism. The criticism also reinforces the impression that the Bush administration did not consider military means as anything like a last resort for dealing with the problem. The attack on Afghanistan was launched within a month of 9/11, which is evidence that the administration chose the military option immediately. Initially dubbing it Operation Infinite Justice, the Pentagon changed the name to Operation Enduring Freedom after religious leaders pointed out that most believers consider that only God can dispense infinite justice.

The Iraq War: Preemptive or Preventive?

Whereas the war in Afghanistan was a response to an attack, the next engagement in the 'war on terror' was not. The US invasion of Iraq in March 2003 was, as US domestic critics such as Senator Edward Kennedy put it, a 'war of choice, not a war of necessity'.[3] The Bush administration prepared the ground for the Iraq War by issuing a major policy document, *The National Security Strategy of the United States of America*, in September 2002. In his covering letter, President Bush asserted that the 'gravest danger our Nation faces lies at the crossroads of radicalism and technology. Our enemies have openly declared that they are seeking weapons of mass destruction, and evidence indicates that they are doing so with determination.' He vowed that, 'as a matter of common sense and self-defense, America will act against such emerging threats before they are fully formed'. Many observers responded by pointing out the great degree of uncertainty inherent in the concept of an 'emerging' threat, not yet 'fully formed'.[4] Moreover, the timing of the document's publication made it appear part of the campaign to justify war against Iraq. Under pressure, Saddam Hussein allowed United Nations specialists to carry out on-site inspections to verify his claim that Iraq was no longer seeking weapons of mass destruction. Even if such weapons existed, Iraq had no means to deliver them at long range. Thus most observers, including many US specialists on international security, deemed the threat posed by Iraq to the United States insufficient to justify claims of self-defense, at least as typically understood.[5]

Traditionally, international law has made a distinction between preemptive attacks and preventive war, and most countries' armed forces accept it. A US Army War College text captures the basic difference in the following definitions:

- Preemptive Attack: An attack or raid initiated on the basis of incontrovertible evidence that an enemy attack is imminent.
- Preventive War: A war initiated in the belief that armed conflict, while not imminent, is inevitable, and that delaying such action would involve unacceptable risk.[6]

Two variables distinguish preemptive from preventive action. The first is *time*. The threat is imminent in the case of preemption, but long-term in the case of prevention. The second variable, related to the first, is *degree of certainty*. The evidence for preemption is 'incontrovertible'. Typical examples would include arming, equipping, and turning on the engines of bomber aircraft, massing of troops on a border, or preparations to launch missiles. Evidence for initiating a preventive war is necessarily more uncertain. Concepts in the US Army definition such as 'inevitable' and 'unacceptable risk' are inherently subjective. A potential enemy's intentions can change with the replacement of government or leadership, for example. Even in the case of Saddam Hussein, although his dictatorship seemed secure, most specialists believed that he could be deterred from aggressive military action through measures far short of preventive war.[7]

The new US strategy posed a particular problem for international law. As the document itself correctly pointed out, 'for centuries, international law recognized that nations need not suffer an attack before they can lawfully take action to defend themselves against forces that present an imminent danger of attack. Legal scholars and international jurists often conditioned the legitimacy of preemption on the existence of an imminent threat – most often a visible mobilization of armies, navies, and air forces preparing to attack.' The new doctrine sought to justify military action in the absence of such visible preparations for attack. As the document put it, 'we must adapt the concept of imminent threat to the capabilities and objectives of today's adversaries', namely – in the category of capabilities – 'acts of terror and, potentially, the use of weapons of mass destruction', and – in the category of objectives – targeting 'our military forces and our civilian population'. If preparation for acts of terror is largely invisible and the use of weapons of mass destruction only 'potential', how could the United States know what or whom to attack? The document does not clarify, but, as every reader recognized, the first target was Iraq.

There are plenty of plausible explanations why the United States invaded Iraq in the face of worldwide opposition and considerable reluctance of its own population. Prominent among them are the strategic goal of securing Middle Eastern oil supplies, the naive idealism of 'democracy promotion' by force of arms, and the greed of private companies, poised to reap a fortune first from the destruction and then from the reconstruction of Iraq. Especially in retrospect, the explanations offered by the Bush administration for going to war – Iraq's possession of weapons of mass destruction and its involvement in the terrorism of 9/11 – seem to make a less convincing *casus belli*. Even at the time, the evidence for a connection between Saddam Hussein and al Qaeda was quite flimsy, with the US Central Intelligence Agency itself, for example, rejecting it.

There seems little doubt that certain officials in the Bush administration came into office intent on war with Iraq, even before 9/11. Nevertheless, the al Qaeda attacks played an important role in allowing for the linguistic and conceptual elision of preemptive and preventive war in the US security doctrine. Moreover, the change in US discourse, carried out in practice in Iraq, could have implications for the development of international law. The next section explores how 9/11 contributed to the invasion of Iraq – a preventive war justified as preemption. The one following it examines the possibility that the newly expanded definition of preemption – and, more significantly, the expansion of the range of conditions that justify resort to armed force – becomes accepted by the 'international community' as a whole.

The 'Cheney Doctrine'

Most accounts of US foreign policy during the early Bush administration accord Vice President Richard Cheney a prominent place, more prominent even than that of the president. Indeed, before the 9/11 attacks, Cheney's role had become the butt of jokes by administration opponents and a source of embarrassment for the Bush White House. Cheney, after all, was the one named by then presidential candidate George W. Bush in 2000 to identify a vice-presidential running mate – and he chose himself. Comedians quipped that if Cheney, who suffered from serious heart disease, were to die suddenly, Bush would become president. It is not surprising that Cheney would have played such an important role in the new administration, especially in foreign policy and in energy policy. The vice-president had vastly more experience than his nominal boss, having served, for example, as a US congressional representative, as White House chief of staff, and as Secretary of Defense, as well as having run unsuccessfully for president. Moreover, when not serving in Washington, Cheney pursued private-sector interests that related directly to US foreign and military policy and to the oil industry.

Indeed, there is a pretty clear relationship between Cheney's government work during the administration of George H. W. Bush and his subsequent financial success. As secretary of defense, Cheney had pursued the privatization of many of the functions of the Pentagon. A major beneficiary of that policy had been the Halliburton Corporation. After Cheney left the Pentagon, he was hired in 1995 as Halliburton's Chief Executive Officer (CEO). The next five years were a period during which, as Joan Didion describes, Cheney 'collected $44 million (plus deferments and stock options) and during which the Halliburton subsidiary Brown & Root had billed the United States $2 billion for services in Bosnia and Kosovo'. Privatization of security functions had gone so far in the Pentagon by the second half of the 1990s that, as CEO Cheney then put it, 'the first person to greet our soldiers as they arrive in the Balkans and the last one to wave goodbye is one of our employees'. With its specialization in energy policy as well as in private security services, Halliburton did very well during the Iraq War, amassing by July 2004 contracts worth $11,431 billion.[8]

The potential conflicts of interest inherent in Cheney's relationship with Halliburton raise ethical and legal questions, but not of the sort that are the focus of this book. Our main interest in the origins of the Iraq War is to evaluate how it conformed to international ethical and legal standards and how it relates to the Global War on Terror. From the perspective of the Bush administration, the first public hint at efforts beyond the immediate task of pursuing the perpetrators of the 9/11 attacks came in the president's speech to a joint session of Congress on 20 September 2001. The president insisted that 'our "war on terror" begins with al Qaeda, but it does not end there. It will not end until every terrorist group of global reach has been found, stopped, and defeated'.[9] So the war began with the pursuit of al Qaeda in Afghanistan the next month, and it continued with the invasion of Iraq in March 2003. How did the Bush administration justify the Iraq War as part of the campaign against international terrorism? This is where the vice-president played a particularly important role.

Publicly, Cheney was the most active Bush administration figure attempting to link Saddam Hussein to al Qaeda. He focused in particular on a meeting he claimed took place in Prague between Mohamed Atta, the 'lead hijacker' of 9/11, and representatives of the Iraqi secret services. Neither US nor Czech intelligence officials believed that such a meeting had taken place. Among other pieces of evidence, the FBI and the CIA had obtained credit-card and phone receipts showing Atta to have been in northern Virginia at the time of the alleged meeting.[10] Nevertheless, Cheney made at least three claims about the connection on NBC television between December 2001 and September 2002. In the first, he asserted that 'it's been pretty well confirmed that [Atta] did go to Prague and he did meet with a senior official of the Iraqi intelligence service in Czechoslovakia [*sic*: = Czech Republic] last April, several months before the attacks'. In March 2002 he referred again to 'the allegation that one of the lead hijackers, Mohamed Atta, had, in fact, met with Iraqi intelligence in Prague'. In September he claimed: 'we have reporting that places [Atta] in Prague with a senior Iraqi intelligence officer a few months before the attacks on the World Trade Center'. Not until March 2006, in an interview with Fox News, did Cheney finally admit that the information he repeatedly provided to the media had been false, all the while denying that his goal in providing it was to link Iraq to al Qaeda: 'We had one report early on from another intelligence service that suggested that the lead hijacker, Mohamed Atta, had met with Iraqi intelligence officials in Prague, Czechoslovakia [*sic*]. And that reporting waxed and waned where the degree of confidence in it, and so forth, has been pretty well knocked down at this stage, that that meeting ever took place. So we've never made the case, or argued the case, that somehow [Saddam Hussein] was directly involved in 9/11. That evidence has never been forthcoming.'[11]

Cheney's interviews were not the only element of the Bush administration's public case linking Iraq to 9/11. The president's own speeches were skillfully constructed to place references to the horror of 9/11 in close juxtaposition to the threat allegedly posed by Saddam Hussein. The media campaign was remarkably effective. A series of polls conducted from June through September 2003, following the initial victory over Saddam Hussein's army, found that 48 percent of the Americans surveyed believed incorrectly that evidence of links between Iraq and al Qaeda had been found; 22 percent believed that invading troops had located weapons of mass destruction in Iraq; and 25 percent believed that public opinion worldwide had supported the US decision to go to war. Overall, 60 percent of those polled reported at least one of these three misperceptions. Those who relied on the Fox television network for news were even more likely to be misinformed. 80 percent of the viewers of Fox reported one of the misperceptions, compared to 23 percent for those who received their news mainly from public television or radio. The president's and vice-president's consistent linking of al Qaeda and Saddam Hussein accounts in part for the misperception reflected in the poll results. What is worse, many US soldiers headed off to war in Iraq literally believing that they were avenging the deaths of 9/11 (85 percent of them, according to one poll), a sentiment with predictably dire consequences for innocent Iraqi civilians.[12]

The link between Iraq and international terrorism was not simply a public relations gambit to justify the March 2003 invasion. That at least is the argument of those, such as Ron Susskind, who link the Iraq War to a near panic within the Bush administration about the prospect of terrorists armed with nuclear or biological weapons. Only a week after the 9/11 attacks, four letters containing anthrax had been sent to US news organizations, followed by similar letters to two US senators. Five people died and a further twenty-three were infected with the anthrax virus. The residents of a tense metropolitan Washington, DC, saw their government agencies and post offices closed. Although an al Qaeda plot was immediately suspected, the FBI soon homed in on a domestic perpetrator. Nevertheless, the following month materials turned up in a bombed al Qaeda site in Afghanistan, documenting the group's interest in using anthrax as a weapon. In the meantime, US intelligence sources were gathering information about a Pakistani organization, known as Islamic Revival, one of whose members was a scientist with connections to Pakistan's nuclear weapons program. From a Libyan source, the CIA learned that the organization had offered to help Libya develop a nuclear bomb.[13]

George Tenet, the Director of Central Intelligence, was particularly keen not to be taken by surprise again, as he had been on 11 September. In Susskind's account he leaned far in the other direction, expecting the worst. Osama bin Laden 'either has a bomb now or won't rest until he has one', he reportedly told a colleague. 'You see, all our failures are because we failed to anticipate. Intelligence failures follow a failure of anticipation. They come from only following the information you know and not worrying about what you don't know. You need to be passionate – passionate *about what you don't know*.'[14]

Tenet's preoccupation with what he did not know – namely, that al Qaeda possessed weapons of mass destruction – played well into the Bush administration's desire to do something 'proactive'. In late November 2001, Tenet briefed the vice-president on the Pakistani group's offer to Libya. 'If there's a one percent chance that Pakistani scientists are helping al Qaeda build or develop a nuclear weapon, we have to treat it as a certainty in terms of our response,' Cheney replied. 'It's not about our analysis, or finding a preponderance of evidence. It's about our response.' As Susskind comments, as far as the *evidence* was concerned, 'the bar was set so low that the word itself almost didn't apply. If there was even a one percent chance of terrorists getting a weapon of mass destruction – and there had been a small probability of such an occurrence for some time – the United States must now act as if it were a certainty. This was a mandate of extraordinary breadth.'[15]

Within that broad mandate, Cheney and the rest of the Bush administration claimed the right to attack Iraq in order to uncover secret programs to develop weapons of mass destruction that could, in turn, be handed over to terrorists who might use them against the United States. Several leaps of faith were necessary for accepting this justification for war. The first one was that Iraq's efforts to develop such weapons had not suffered irreparably from the previous war in 1991, from the UN inspections, which uncovered and destroyed many of the relevant facilities, or from the regime of economic sanctions, which aimed to deny Iraq any material linked – even plausibly – to the production of weapons. The second leap consisted in believing that secular Iraq would share whatever weapons it had developed with an organization of religiously motivated fanatics like al Qaeda. The third – that, if it nevertheless did so and al Qaeda carried out an attack against the United States, Iraq's role could go undetected and unpunished by retaliation. In effect, the Bush administration was willing to make those leaps of faith and to punish Iraq in advance, denying it the opportunity – however implausible – to contribute to a terrorist attack against the United States with weapons of mass destruction.

In January 2002, in his State of the Union address, President Bush announced his goal 'to prevent regimes that sponsor terror from threatening America or our friends and allies with weapons of mass destruction'. He devoted to North Korea and to Iran a brief sentence each, and then he turned to Iraq:

> Iraq continues to flaunt its hostility toward America and to support terror. The Iraqi regime has plotted to develop anthrax, and nerve gas, and nuclear weapons for over a decade. This is a regime that has already used poison gas to murder thousands of its own citizens – leaving the bodies of mothers huddled over their dead children. This is a regime that agreed to international inspections – then kicked out the inspectors. This is a regime that has something to hide from the civilized world.
>
> States like these, and their terrorist allies, constitute an axis of evil, arming to threaten the peace of the world. By seeking weapons of mass destruction, these regimes pose a grave and growing danger. They could provide these arms to terrorists, giving them the means to match their hatred. They could attack our allies or attempt to blackmail the United States. In any of these cases, the price of indifference would be catastrophic.[16]

This was the Bush–Cheney brief for launching preventive war against Iraq.

Revising US National Security Doctrine

In June 2002, President George W. Bush made a speech at the US Military Academy at West Point in which he claimed: 'if we wait for threats to fully materialize, we will have waited too long'. The editors of *Air Force Magazine* correctly described Bush's remarks as announcing a ' "preventive war" concept', something that 'went well beyond "anticipatory self-defense' ", and which some could see 'as the equivalent of Japan's December 1941 attack on Pearl Harbor'.[17] Three months later, in September 2002, the National Security Strategy document would seek to redefine the preventive motive as preemption.

> The United States has long maintained the option of pre-emptive actions to counter a sufficient threat to our national security. The greater the threat, the greater is the risk of inaction – and the more compelling the case for taking anticipatory action to defend ourselves, even if uncertainty remains as to the time and place of the enemy's attack. To forestall or prevent such hostile acts by our adversaries, the United States will, if necessary, act preemptively.[18]

Two key points are worth stressing here. First, the US government sought deliberately to conflate preemption and prevention by expanding the time horizon and by underplaying the degree of certainty necessary to justify preventive war. In order to 'prevent' hostile acts, the United States will 'act preemptively'. The second key point is found in the phrase 'the greater the threat, the greater is the risk of inaction'. If the threat is mass civilian casualties caused by terrorist use of nuclear weapons, the US clearly must *do something*, because inaction is too risky.

Even though the theme of acting in anticipation of uncertain
threats resembles what Susskind dubbed 'the Cheney doctrine', the main credit for the National Security Strategy
document is generally accorded to Condoleezza Rice, the president's national security adviser at the time. She assigned the
task of drafting the document to her friend and colleague,
Philip Zelikow.[19] Both Rice and Zelikow knew the difference
between prevention and preemption, so one can assume that
their conflation of the two was deliberate. During the Cold War,
working as a professor of political science and specialist in
international security, Rice would have insisted that her students at Stanford understand the difference between preventive and preemptive wars. It was a bread-and-butter issue in
courses on nuclear strategy, for example. If the United States
had, during the period of its 'atomic monopoly' from 1945 to
1949, carried out an attack against the Soviet Union, in order
to destroy that country's ability to produce nuclear weapons
years before there was any evidence of the latter's intent to produce any, that would have been a preventive war. If, having
achieved a nuclear capability, the Soviet Union had tried to
launch a secret attack 'out of the blue', but the United States
had detected it and attacked first, that attack would have
been characterized as 'preemption' and plausibly justified on
grounds of anticipatory self-defense.

Fortunately, Soviet leaders never contemplated such a
'nuclear Pearl Harbor' and President Harry Truman rejected
proposals for preventive war against the USSR. Nevertheless,
students of international security during the Cold War were
obliged to answer exam questions about preventive and preemptive attacks, and their professors, such as Condoleezza
Rice, were equally obliged to know the difference. Philip
Zelikow, who taught for a time at Harvard's Kennedy School
of Government, and who co-authored the revised edition of
Graham Allison's classic book on the Cuban Missile Crisis,

Essence of Decision, certainly knew the difference.[20] Much of the study of nuclear strategy focused on the instability inherent in a relationship where each side might be tempted to launch an attack, out of fear of the devastating consequences of a preemptive strike by the other side. Yet the leaders of the nuclear powers appeared to recognize the risks of making a mistake and of attacking an adversary who had no intention to attack first. Thus, the fabled 'balance of terror' remained stable enough to forestall catastrophe.

The Bush administration's officials – products of the Cold War par excellence – nevertheless neglected to foresee the consequences of their precipitate invasion of Iraq. They seemed unaware that over a hundred years of US efforts at 'regime change' by military force had yielded, at best, mixed results and, in the evaluation of one important study, unintended consequences that usually weakened US security.[21] Especially surprising is the impression that veteran officials such as Cheney forgot the very reasons they themselves had identified for not seeking to depose Saddam Hussein in 1991. In April 1991, for example, the *New York Times* reported then Secretary of Defense Cheney's reasons. In his words,

> If you're going to go in and try to topple Saddam Hussein, you have to go to Baghdad. Once you've got Baghdad, it's not clear what you do with it. It's not clear what kind of government you would put in place of the one that's currently there now. Is it going to be a Shia regime, a Sunni regime or a Kurdish regime? Or one that tilts toward the Baathists, or one that tilts toward the Islamic fundamentalists? How much credibility is that government going to have if it's set up by the United States military when it's there? How long does the United States military have to stay to protect the people that sign on for that government, and what happens to it once we leave?[22]

A few years later, Cheney elaborated on the argument about the chaos that would attend a US occupation of Iraq for a documentary film on the 1991 war. In 1996, after taking over as head of Halliburton, Cheney presented further reasons for not seeking to overthrow Saddam Hussein, at that time a potential customer for his firm:

> [I]f Saddam wasn't there, his successor probably wouldn't be notably friendlier to the United States than he is. I also look at that part of the world as of vital interest to the United States; for the next hundred years it's going to be the world's supply of oil. We've got a lot of friends in the region. We're always going to have to be involved there. Maybe it's part of our national character, you know, we like to have these problems nice and neatly wrapped up, put a ribbon around it.

Cheney concluded with a particularly prescient remark: 'You deploy a force, you win the war, and the problem goes away, and it doesn't work that way in the Middle East; it never has *and isn't likely to in my lifetime.*'[23]

Despite the many still relevant reasons not to launch a war for 'regime change' in Iraq, Cheney became one of the strongest proponents of just such a course of action. One key difference between the early 1990s and a decade later was the impact of 9/11 on policy-makers. The al Qaeda attacks had shown them to be vulnerable and incompetent to defend their country. They were determined to do something forceful, to show that they were in charge. In that respect, Iraq was an appealing target not because it was strong and menacing, but rather because it was weak. Secretary of Defense Donald Rumsfeld saw Iraq as an ideal opportunity to demonstrate his preferred strategy of relying on technology to limit the need for massive numbers of soldiers.[24]

The number of potential targets for a preventive war is typically greater than for a preemptive attack. Immediate, certain threats are likely to be fewer than distant, uncertain ones. Why, then, did the Bush administration choose to attack Iraq? If the goal was to disrupt ties between terrorist organizations and nuclear weapons facilities, Pakistan would have been a more obvious choice. If the point was to punish countries that had provided safe haven to al Qaeda, there were several candidates after Afghanistan, with clearer connections than the one suggested by the spurious meeting in Prague between Mohamed Atta and an Iraq intelligence official. Saudi Arabia was an obvious choice, and the Federal Republic of Germany another. After all, much of the plotting of the 9/11 attacks took place in Hamburg.

Yet Iraq had long been in the gun sights of many in the Bush administration, and here the relevance of 9/11 is less significant. Paul Wolfowitz, deputy secretary of defense under Rumsfeld, had worked on Iraq going back as far as the administration of James E. Carter. Then Secretary of Defense Harold Brown had commissioned Wolfowitz to draft a study on 'Capabilities for limited contingencies in the Persian Gulf', in which Wolfowitz and his co-author, Dennis Ross, had conjured a threat from the Soviet Union to the oil resources of the Middle East and had planned a US military response. They also imagined that Iraq might attack Saudi Arabia or Kuwait and, with control over vast reserves of oil, emerge as the dominant power in the region. Secretary Brown found the scenario too implausible, but Wolfowitz insisted to Ross that, '[w]hen you look at contingencies, you don't focus only on the likelihood of the contingency but also on the severity of its consequences'.[25] If the consequences of even an implausible scenario are severe enough, the scenario in question is worth planning for. Wolfowitz's thinking bears considerable resemblance to the 'one percent doctrine' attributed to Cheney, so it is not surprising that the two found a common cause in the invasion of Iraq in 2003. For Wolfowitz, however, the early concern about Iraq was not a function of his desire to promote democracy there or something related to Saddam Hussein's brutal rule. As James Mann explains, 'at this juncture in the

late 1970s, when Wolfowitz first began to focus his attention
upon Iraq, Saddam Hussein had not yet had time to consoli-
date his control over the leadership, to repress all dissent in the
country or to use chemical weapons against Iraq's Kurdish
population. Wolfowitz's earliest interest in Iraq, then, arose
from concerns about oil, geopolitics and the balance of power
in the Persian Gulf, not from concerns about Saddam
Hussein's behavior.'[26]

Between the Wolfowitz/Ross study of June 1979 and Iraq's
actual invasion of Kuwait in August 1990, the geopolitics of
the gulf changed dramatically. Saddam Hussein's armies
attacked Iran in September 1980, attempting to take advantage of the new revolutionary regime's assumed weakness
and to settle a territorial dispute. At that point, the United
States was tacitly backing the Iraqi side. US support for the
brutal dictatorship of the Shah of Iran had made it unlikely
that the successor regime of Islamic clerics would view the
United States with anything but hostility. The seizure of the
US embassy in Tehran by revolutionary students, endorsed as
it was by the new regime, assured that the United States, in
turn, would view the new Iran as an enemy. Employing the
maxim 'the enemy of my enemy is my friend', the United
States and its European and Middle Eastern allies supplied
Saddam Hussein's regime with arms and with ingredients
necessary to create a chemical weapons industry. Declassified
US government documents offer extensive evidence of US
support for Iraq, especially in the early years of the war. In
1983, President Ronald Reagan sent Donald Rumsfeld as his
special envoy to Baghdad, where he shook Saddam Hussein's
hand and discussed matters of mutual interest. The following
year, the CIA began providing Iraq with satellite intelligence,
to coordinate its chemical weapons attacks against Iran.[27]
Relations were sufficiently amicable in subsequent years for
Saddam Hussein to believe, evidently, that he had received a

green light from US Ambassador April Glaspie in 1990 for his invasion of Kuwait. The strong US reaction and the assembly of a multinational coalition to remove Iraq's army from Kuwait marked a turning point in US–Iraqi relations and set the stage for later confrontations, which culminated in the March 2003 invasion.

Preventive War and the Evolution of International Law

I suggested above that the new US strategy of preventive war in the guise of preemption posed a problem for international law. Why did international law – with its clear distinction of principle between preventive and preemptive military action – not pose a problem for the US strategy? Bush administration officials did not concern themselves much about international law because they did not consider themselves bound by it – or not by much of it. As the previous chapter's discussion of torture and the mistreatment of detainees has established, many members of the administration held the view that the president's constitutionally designated role as commander-in-chief of the armed forces put him even above domestic law. A novelty for the Bush administration was the extension of executive privilege to the vice-president. As Joan Didion describes, 'since November 1, 2001, under this administration's Executive Order 13233, which limits access to all presidential and vice-presidential papers, Cheney has been the first vice-president in American history entitled to executive privilege, a claim to co-presidency reinforced in March 2003 by Executive Order 13292, giving him the same power to classify information as the president has'.[28] Acting unconstrained by domestic US law, Cheney presumably felt little constraint from international law as he advocated a preventive war that most of the world understood as illegal.

Given the widespread opposition to the US-led war in Iraq, one might expect that the norm against preventive war would be strengthened in response. Prominent violations of a well-established norm, if met with strong condemnation, often do serve to reinforce it. In this case, however, the response of other states and international and nongovernmental organizations to the US invasion and occupation of Iraq was more ambivalent. Although the United Nations Security Council refused to endorse the invasion, it did effectively endorse the occupation. The United Nations Assistance Mission for Iraq (UNAMI), for example, was established on 14 August 2003, to aid in post-war reconstruction. Security Council Resolution 1546 (adopted unanimously in June 2004), in the summary provided by the US-run Coalition Provisional Authority (CPA), 'endorses the new interim government of Iraq, allows the multinational force to provide security in partnership with the new government, sets out a leading role for the UN in helping the political process over the next year, and calls upon the international community to aid Iraq in its transition'. The council also indicated in the document's opening paragraph that it was '*looking forward* to the end of the occupation and the assumption of full responsibility and authority by a fully sovereign and independent Interim Government of Iraq by 30 June 2004' – a fact not mentioned in the CPA's summary introduction. The Security Council subsequently issued extensions of its endorsement of the continued presence of foreign troops, as Iraq failed to achieve sovereign status.[29]

In international law, some practices are understood to have 'a peremptory or *jus cogens* character, such as the most fundamental of human rights or the prohibition against aggression'.[30] Even if states have not signed a specific treaty agreeing to abide by such a prohibition, they are considered bound by customary law. There is no legal option of *derogation*, or non-compliance with part of the law. States can change customary law, however, by their *practice*. Practice in this sense does not mean only obvious actions, such as the use of military force. In the realm of international humanitarian law, for example, an important judgment related to the wars in former Yugoslavia, known as the Tadić Case, explained that 'in appraising the formation of customary rules or general principles . . . reliance must primarily be placed on such elements as official pronouncements of States, military manuals and judicial discussions'.[31] If states intend to reaffirm customary law prohibitions such as the norm against preventive war, they should act accordingly. When the members of the Security Council implicitly endorsed the US invasion and occupation of Iraq by approving the actions of the Coalition Provisional Authority and the continued presence of foreign troops, they missed an opportunity to stigmatize a practice that many of them had claimed, before the invasion, to consider illegal. Of course, other factors than the status of preventive war under customary law came into consideration in the Security Council's deliberations – such as whether there were any alternatives for Iraq better than the continuing foreign occupation.

It is conceivable that the Security Council's actions did not constitute simply a tough choice that unintentionally failed to stigmatize the practice of preventive war in Iraq. On the contrary, it could be seen as consistent with what some observers have called an 'emerging consensus for preventive war'. Peter Dombrowski and Rodger Payne have gathered considerable evidence of the sort that the Tadić? Case ruling suggests should be relevant: in particular, official pronouncements by various states and international bodies on the acceptability of preventive military action for certain purposes. First, they point out that, by the calculations of the Bush administration, forty-eight countries supported the invasion of Iraq, even if far fewer actually provided any military contribution. The prime ministers of Australia, the United Kingdom, and Italy came out with explicit statements of support for the US interpretation of a right of preemption.

Second, several others countries facing terrorist threats of the sort that the United States imagined to emanate from Iraq vowed to pursue preventive measures to deal with them. Israel threatened preventive action to forestall Iran's acquisition of nuclear weapons, and it had the power of precedent to back up that threat: In 1981 Israeli air forces had destroyed Iraq's Osirak reactor using the same justification. Indian Defense Minister George Fernandes similarly threatened neighboring Pakistan. He also implicitly supported the discursive ploy adopted by the United States – to blur the distinction between prevention and preemption – by using the latter to mean the former. He claimed, for example, that, 'more than Iraq, Pakistan is a fit case to launch pre-emptive strikes'.[32] Russian President Vladimir Putin declared that his country also favored preventive action, that it had the right to attack neighboring states such as Georgia or Ukraine if it found that they were harboring terrorists who might pose a threat to the Russian Federation. The chief of the Russian General Staff went even further, indicating that Russia could launch preemptive strikes on terrorist bases anywhere. 'Speaking of preemptive strikes,' he said, 'Russia will take all necessary steps for destroying terrorist bases in any part of the world. However,' he added reassuringly, 'it does not mean that we are going to use nuclear weapons during counterterrorist operations.'[33] The Bush administration, by contrast, advocated creating a new type of nuclear weapon, the so-called Robust Nuclear Earth Penetrator, precisely in order to destroy deep underground facilities which might harbor terrorists or weapons of mass destruction.[34] If the norm of preventive war seemed to be catching on internationally, its nuclear variant remained less popular.

The third piece of evidence for preventive war as an emerging norm consists of documents issued by international organizations such as the United Nations, the European Union, and the North Atlantic Treaty Organization. They appear to entertain, if not fully endorse, measures of preventive military action to deal with the joint threats of terrorism and of weapons of mass destruction. The High-Level Panel on Threats, Challenges and Change, an international body of experts convened by the UN General Secretary, offers a good example. In its report, issued in 2004, the panel argued that 'in the world of the twenty-first century, the international community does have to be concerned about nightmare scenarios combining terrorists, weapons of mass destruction, and irresponsible states and much more besides, which may conceivably justify the use of force, not just reactively but preventively and before a latent threat becomes imminent'.[35]

Can we argue, then, that the US war on terror and the way the Bush administration sought to put it into practice, through a preventive war against Iraq, contributed to an evolution in international law? Is preventive war now considered more acceptable than it was in the past? Is it no longer considered a violation of customary law? The safe – and correct – answer is that it is too early to tell. International legal scholars and political scientists have produced excellent work seeking to establish the conditions and factors that influence the formation and erosion of customary norms. But there is still basic disagreement on such fundamental questions as 'how many states have to validate a new norm before it can be said to have acquired the status of a new rule of customary international law'.[36] Moreover, as we have seen, there is more to the formulation of customary law than the behavior of states. State practice is only one component. Another is *opinio iuris sive necessitatis*, or, for short, *opinio iuris*, what Price defines as 'the belief by states that the practice is undertaken as an obligation of international law'. Do states believe that preventive war has now become accepted practice, legally sanctioned, or do they see such actions as exceptional, given the particularly grave combination of terrorist threats, 'failed states', and weapons of mass destruction? For, as Price points out, 'when extreme circumstances are invoked to justify a departure, or when attempts are made to conceal violations, violations are less harmful to the overall persistence of a norm and the norm can be said to be more robust, than situations in which norms are violated more as a matter of course'.[37] Is the norm restricting military action to self-defense still robust, or is it being undermined by state practice such as the US invasion of Iraq? Do expressions of support for preventive action constitute *opinio iuris* or do they reflect an exceptional circumstance?

Attempts to answer these questions are complicated by the fact that states and individuals disagree on what constitutes preventive action. In considering prevention and preemption, a number of international organizations sought, for example, to broaden the concept beyond military means. For NATO and the European Union, for example, one can perhaps even identify a 'uniquely European style of preemption: preemption of the formation or acceptance of terrorist ideologies and cells in the world's poorest regions through early crisis intervention and peace-keeping, humanitarian aid, and nation building activities'.[38] If preventive measures include such non-military means of forestalling the rise of terrorist threats, and come gradually to eliminate the perceived need for preventive wars, that would allow the self-defense norm to remain robust while allowing states to cope with the new threats that face them.

Even if military force remains a major instrument for the prevention of terrorism, the legality of its use can depend on particular circumstances. The most common distinction is between unilateral use of force by one state or coalition of states (a 'coalition of the willing', as the Bush administration put it), without official sanction by the United Nations, and a multilateral action undertaken in accordance with the Security Council's authority under Chapter VII. The latter is understood to stand on firmer legal ground. If Security Council authorization for anti-terrorist preventive war became the norm, the prevailing customary rule limiting the use of force to self-defense might survive. Nevertheless, the consequences of UN-sanctioned preventive war might be no different from those that result from the actions of a single state or coalition. There would still be the uncertainty inherent in using military force against a threat which had not yet emerged and might not ever fully emerge in the future. Neta Crawford has referred to this as the difference between an *imminent* threat that could justify preemption and an *immanent* threat – a general sense of anxiety about a dangerous world and hostile adversaries who may become potential targets for preventive war but pose no immediate threat.[39]

If the Security Council came to authorize preventive military actions, or enough states engaged in them on a regular basis, we might say that preventive war has become legal. In the former situation, military action would still require the Security Council's authority on a case-by-case basis, whereas in the latter state practice would constitute a new norm of customary law. In either case, the ethical status of preventive war would still be in doubt. Ethical considerations do not always line up with legal ones. Of particular concern in preventive wars is the damage to innocent civilians. The most striking case is the war in Iraq. According to the most careful analysis of violent civilian deaths since the US invasion, the numbers by mid-2006 fell in the range of 600,000, on the basis of a large scientific sampling of Iraqi households. Between March 2003 and July 2006, household surveys attributed 31 percent of deaths to the US-led coalition forces, thereafter dropping to 26 percent. In addition to the numbers of deaths, one should also consider the refugee crisis that the war precipitated, with some 2 million Iraqis having fled their country and a further 2.2 million internally displaced.[40]

In assessing the morality of the invasion of Iraq, one would use the just war principle of *reasonable hope* (discussed in Chapter 1) to assess whether the civilian deaths were in any sense 'worth it'. First, one would have to clarify the goals of the invasion – a problematic task, given how many different ones the Bush administration offered at any given time: deposing Saddam Hussein, destroying Iraq's weapons of mass destruction, bringing democracy to the Middle East, preventing another 9/11. Some of those goals were incapable of achievement. Following years of economic sanctions and UN inspections, there were no weapons of mass destruction left to discover or destroy, for example. Democratizing the Middle East is not a goal that anyone should reasonably have hoped to achieve through a military invasion, and few expect to see a democratic Iraq any time soon. Most assessments, including a 2006 National Intelligence Estimate summarizing the views of 16 US intelligence agencies, suggest that the risk of terrorism has increased rather than declined as a result of the war in Iraq – a finding that confirms the pre-war predictions of many critics of the Bush administration.[41] Of those goals, the only one clearly achieved was removing Saddam Hussein from power. Was deposing and executing him worth the deaths of hundreds of thousands of Iraqi civilians? Those are the kinds of questions that policy-makers contemplating future preventive wars will need to ask themselves – especially if they intend to justify the wars on humanitarian grounds, the topic of the next chapter.

This chapter has reviewed the main justifications offered for the US-led wars in Afghanistan and Iraq. The first was widely accepted as a war of self-defense, waged in response to the terrorist attacks of September 2001. The Bush administration also offered humanitarian motives for the Afghan War, as the next chapter discusses in more detail, but such motives were not necessary for the war to receive the endorsement of the United Nations Security Council and the North Atlantic Treaty Alliance. The Bush administration sought to justify its 2003 invasion of Iraq on numerous grounds. This chapter focused on the efforts, led by Vice President Cheney, to characterize the war as a preventive effort to destroy the potential threat that terrorists would obtain weapons of mass destruction from Iraq to use against the United States and its allies. Then it reviewed evidence suggesting that, despite the widespread international opposition to the invasion of Iraq itself, there is considerable sympathy for preventive action to forestall terrorist attacks. If such action becomes understood to include a major military component, we could be witnessing the emergence of a new norm of preventive war and the undermining of the traditional norm that military forces should be used only in self-defense against aggression and imminent attack.

CHAPTER FIVE

Humanitarian Objectives in Anti-Terror Wars

This chapter addresses the unusual nature of the actual wars fought as part of the Global War on Terror. Among other things, the military campaigns in Afghanistan and Iraq were justified as efforts to overthrow the evil regimes led by the Taliban and Saddam Hussein, respectively, in the interest of ordinary Afghans and Iraqis. 'Regime change' as a component of the war on terror poses particular problems for international law and for the behavior of international and nongovernmental organizations. Traditional law of military occupation assumes minimal changes to the political and economic structure of a defeated belligerent, in anticipation of a return to the *status quo ante*. Agencies of the United Nations, the International Committee of the Red Cross (ICRC), and nongovernmental humanitarian aid organizations premise their involvement in such situations on their neutrality and on their immunity from attack. Yet if they become involved in reconstruction efforts, especially in an environment where portions of the population remain hostile to the intentions of the occupying power, as is the case in Iraq, they appear implicitly to be taking sides. The war on terror has only sharpened the ethical dilemma that humanitarian aid organizations have faced since the end of the Cold War.

'Humanitarian intervention' poses ethical and legal challenges to states as well. As with earlier wars promoted on humanitarian grounds, such as NATO's interventions in

Bosnia and Kosovo, the humanitarian motives in the Afghan and Iraq Wars led to a paradoxical situation. The intervening states' apparent sympathy for the civilian population should lead them to take extra precautions to protect it during the prosecution of the war and the subsequent military occupation. On the other hand, if the political leaders justify the wars by reference to altruistic motives rather than to national interest, they may find it difficult to permit any unnecessary risk to their own country's soldiers. Such political considerations seem to have encouraged the use of several practices to minimize danger to the soldiers of the intervening forces, at the expense of risking greater harm to innocent civilians: 'subcontracting' to local forces such as the Kosovo Liberation Army or the Northern Alliance in Afghanistan, or to private military corporations, thereby increasing the likelihood of, and obscuring the responsibility for, abuses of civilians; reliance on aerial bombardment, with the attendant prospect of 'collateral damage' instead of the riskier deployment of soldiers on the ground; widespread destruction of infrastructure (such as electricity grids, bridges, water and sewage treatment facilities) which could serve military purposes, but is also essential for civilian survival. The laws of war offer little clarity about how to deal with these issues that bear on the protection of civilians.

This chapter begins with an overview of the military interventions conducted on humanitarian grounds starting in the 1990s. Although these conflicts predate the Global War on Terror, for nongovernmental proponents of peace and human rights they posed many of the ethical and practical dilemmas that took on crisis proportions with the US-led invasion of Iraq in March 2003. The chapter summarizes the main issues that face nongovernmental organizations and then turns to the legal and ethical questions that implicate states, and, in particular, the USA.

Paradoxes of Humanitarian War

The humanitarian impulse that inspired Henry Dunant and his Swiss colleagues to found the International Committee of the Red Cross continues to motivate efforts to relieve the suffering that war and atrocity bring about. Paradoxically, war itself has often served as the instrument for relieving that suffering. The emblematic example is World War II and the military campaigns that brought an end to the tyrannical Nazi regime, which had killed and enslaved millions. A further paradox is that humanitarian organizations, such as the ICRC, consider that they can be most effective if they do not choose sides in a conflict. The principles of *impartiality* and *neutrality* are what allows Red Cross workers to provide medical care on the battlefield and to civilians caught up in war – the issue that drove Dunant's earliest efforts, following the searing experience of Solferino. The Red Cross is supposed to offer its services, equally, to the wounded of all sides, on the basis of need and in ways that do not give one side a military advantage. In order for such organizations to function, they depend on a further principle, *inviolability*: 'the assurance that their personnel, their property, and their activities will not be made the object of attack'.[1]

The traditional attitude of the ICRC towards war also appears paradoxical. In the words of Caroline Moorhead, under its mandate the Red Cross movement 'could protest against the horrors of war, do all in its power to mitigate its most murderous aspect, but it could not lobby actively against war itself, even if some of the national societies that made up its membership were actively in favour of pacifism'.[2] In its view, the International Committee could not denounce the resort to war, for instance when Japan invaded and ravaged Manchuria in 1931, when Italy provoked war with Ethiopia in 1935, or when Germany launched its *Blitzkrieg* against Poland in 1939; nor could it champion war as a means to defeat these aggressor states. Its approach to war is consistent with the many contradictory aspects of its identity. In David Forsythe's characterization, the ICRC 'espouses liberal ends but conservative means, championing the worth of the individual but proceeding cautiously on the basis of state consent – which can be slow to manifest itself'.[3]

Maintaining strict neutrality in the face of such an obvious evil as Nazism discredited the ICRC in the eyes of many observers. The ideological polarization of the Cold War constituted an equally inhospitable environment for the work of the Red Cross and kindred organizations. There was not much middle ground between those who characterized the conflict as pitting totalitarian communism against liberal democracy and those who preferred, instead, to think of it as a struggle of national liberation and people's democracy against rapacious imperialism and militarism.

The end of the Cold War offered a possibility for greater consensus in international life, to the extent that one observer declared the End of History and another – the first President George Bush – spoke of a New World Order.[4] Bush's inspiration was the decision taken by the United Nations Security Council to oppose Iraq's invasion and occupation of Kuwait in August 1990; his characterization seemed vindicated when that body authorized military action in February 1991, to reverse the Iraqi invasion. Erstwhile adversaries cooperated to enforce bedrock principles of the United Nations Charter: the prohibition against military aggression and the inviolability of sovereign borders. The seeming consensus on fundamental international principles did not make the task of humanitarian aid organizations necessarily easier. In a conflict between a unified international community and a pariah state, were they still supposed to maintain neutrality?

The dilemma facing the aid organizations surfaced most starkly in the debates during the 1990s over humanitarian intervention. Adam Roberts defines the phrase as 'coercive action by one or more states involving the use of armed force in another state without the consent of its authorities, and with the purpose of preventing widespread suffering or death among the inhabitants'.[5] Humanitarian intervention poses a dilemma because it engages two sets of values held by most members of aid organizations. One set opposes state violence and military force. The other supports the security and wellbeing of individuals. Humanitarian intervention entails supporting state violence in the interest of protecting individuals. The tension between these values for individuals and organizations that favor both peace and human rights is evident.

The 1990s witnessed several opportunities, many of them missed or botched, for the use of military force to prevent mass atrocities. In 1992, a UN-sanctioned and US-led intervention into Somalia, initially designed (and with some success) to relieve a famine, evolved into active participation in an internal conflict and then into a quick retreat after the deaths of eighteen US soldiers (and hundreds of Somali civilians). The Somali disaster contributed to reluctance on the part of the major powers to intervene to halt the genocide in Rwanda two years later, although the French sent troops belatedly, after perhaps 800,000 people had already perished. The break-up of Yugoslavia in the early 1990s led to widespread violence against civilians, especially in Bosnia, but the United States and its allies were unwilling to intervene until hundreds of thousands of people had been killed or expelled.

Much as the lesson learned from Somalia (with dire consequences for Rwanda) was not to intervene, Rwanda and Bosnia created their own set of lessons and a compulsion to intervene before small-scale massacres turned into genocide. When Serb militia and Yugoslav army forces began terrorizing and expelling ethnic Albanians (the vast majority of the population) in the formerly autonomous province of Kosovo, the

United States and its allies took action. The North Atlantic Treaty Organization launched its first war in March 1999, ostensibly in support of UN resolutions that Serbia had failed to implement, but without express UN Security Council authorization. Justified as a humanitarian operation intended to save the lives of Kosovar Albanians, the war entailed large-scale aerial bombardment of Serbia proper, including the capital city, Belgrade. Serb forces took advantage of the war to escalate violence against civilians, killing some 10,000 before the war ended on 19 June 1999. Between the Serb violence and the NATO bombing, an estimated 863,000 Kosovars fled the country and a further 590,000 were internally displaced.[6]

During the Cold War, humanitarian groups and peace activists had often criticized US support of dictatorial regimes, armed intervention in places like Vietnam and Central America, and military policies that risked nuclear war. The wars in former Yugoslavia constituted only one set of cases where some of these groups felt inclined to change their attitudes toward US power. As one US representative of Human Rights Watch put it in the summer of 2001, 'in the past US activists were concerned about preventing the US from doing harm. Now they are concerned about keeping the US engaged and trying to construct nationally based international arguments to justify humanitarian [military] activities.'[7] The US-led war on terror has driven many human rights activists back into an adversarial stance, but humanitarian aid groups are still heavily implicated in US foreign policy priorities, including the wars that create as well as relieve humanitarian crises.

The war in Iraq offers the most dramatic evidence of the risks facing humanitarian aid organizations. In August 2003, barely half a year after the US-led invasion, opponents of the subsequent military occupation bombed the United Nations headquarters in Iraq, killing twenty-three people, including Sergio Vieira de Mello, the special representative of the secretary general. Two months later, an ambulance packed with explosives slammed into the Baghdad compound of the ICRC, killing eighteen civilian bystanders and wounding dozens more. Nicolas de Torrenté, the executive director of the US branch of Médecins sans Frontières (Doctors without Borders), pointed out that the ICRC was unusual among aid organizations in that it had 'a long history of providing assistance in Iraq'. During the Iran–Iraq war, it played its traditional role of caring for prisoners of war, and it maintained a presence throughout the 1991 Gulf War, throughout the long years of economic sanctions that followed, and into the 2003 war. If the United Nations, the representative of all countries, and the International Committee of the Red Cross, the preeminent neutral and impartial aid organization, could no longer enjoy inviolability, could any humanitarian groups expect it? In the wake of the attacks, many organizations withdrew from Iraq, prompting de Torrenté to ask the question: 'Do aid organizations have choices left other than to seek armed protection and to work in full cooperation with Western military and political forces or simply retreat?'[8]

What makes situations like the occupation of Iraq so dangerous for humanitarian organizations? For one thing, the goals of the organizations are increasingly at odds with those of many of the people carrying out the violence. International humanitarian law (IHL) emerged in an era when wars were supposed to be fought between the armed forces of states, avoiding harm to civilians to the extent that that was possible. States accordingly allowed the Red Cross workers to tend to noncombatants: civilians, wounded soldiers, and prisoners of war. In the 'new wars' of the post-Cold War era, this model rarely applies. As de Torrenté points out, 'as is so often the case today, wars are fought *over*, rather than around civilians. While IHL seeks to remove noncombatants from the equation, warring parties are increasingly placing them at its center.'[9] This trend predates the war on terror by many years. The war in Bosnia in the mid-1990s, for example, was not, as foreign governments and media sought to portray it, a civil war pitting the armed forces of one side against those of the other, with civilians caught in between. As one authoritative account explains, 'the columns of refugees that spilled into Croatia in April and May 1992 were not fleeing the war zones. They had been driven from their homes on the grounds of their nationality. They were not the tragic by-product of a civil war; their expulsion was the whole point of the war.'[10]

Increasingly in the wars and humanitarian crises of the 1990s, aid groups seeking to provide relief to civilians at risk found it difficult to maintain neutrality and impartiality – or, at least, the consequences of their efforts were not neutral, and were not what they intended. Aid groups would find, for example, that food distributed at refugee camps ends up under the control of militia leaders, who divert it to their soldiers. Or, if humanitarian workers delivered supplies to civilian populations that a certain militia group considered the enemy, the workers themselves would become targets of violence.[11] Such difficulties are endemic to any conflict where the control or destruction of civilians is the objective.

That humanitarian aid organizations might not enjoy inviolability in a war on terror was evident even before 9/11. In 1999, the United Kingdom apparently harbored such concerns, as the United States sought to promote a UN Security Council resolution to threaten sanctions against the Taliban regime if it did not turn over Osama bin Laden. Although Britain voted for the resolution, it reportedly feared a backlash against UN and private agencies providing aid in Afghanistan. The World Food Organization did remove its staff from the country, whereas the ICRC remained. A German aid organization which remained witnessed the arrest of twenty-six of its workers. Similar arrests of aid workers accused of breaking their commitment to impartiality came in the wake of the NATO war in Kosovo.[12]

When the United States invaded Afghanistan in 2001 to overthrow the Taliban regime and pursue al Qaeda, its justification on grounds of self-defense received widespread support from the United Nations Security Council, the North Atlantic Treaty Organization, and other international bodies. The Bush administration nevertheless chose to portray the war as serving humanitarian purposes as well – including, as First Lady Laura Bush was recruited to emphasize, the liberation of Afghan women.[13]

In the case of the Iraq War, the prominent role of the United States created difficulties for the aid organizations. As de Torrenté argued, 'the manner in which the US-led coalition made the minimization of harm and the provision of relief for Iraqis an integral part of its political and military agenda contributed significantly to the hostility towards humanitarian action and those who deliver it'.[14] This assessment understates the extent to which the US occupation itself generated ill will among ordinary Iraqis. Phillip Walker offers an important reminder of what war and military occupation mean in the absence of law:

> Foreign military occupation remains one of the most terrifying events that can befall a nation, precisely because individuals under occupation are at the mercy of armed foreigners. Between occupier and occupied, no social contract exists. Absent application of the laws of war, only personal morality prevents individual soldiers from looting, raping, torturing, or killing at will. The old maxim that power corrupts applies both to privates and presidents, and in an occupation setting, every private is a dictator to those within his grasp.

Actual examples of the hypothetical violations that Walker enumerates – looting, raping, torturing, and killing at will – have been well documented in Iraq. As Walker suggests, they stem from a larger fundamental violation of the laws of war, in this case the law of belligerent occupation. The Coalition Provisional Authority (CPA) set up by the United States to run Iraq 'took an expansive view of its own authority' which 'conflicted with the limited nature of occupation described by the Fourth Geneva Convention and the Hague Regulations'. In particular, the CPA failed to maintain basic public order and initiated profound economic and legal changes to the Iraqi system – actions consistent with a mission of 'regime change', but clear violations of international law.[15] The daily brutalization of, and disrespect towards, ordinary Iraqis at the hands of foreign soldiers could not help but reflect poorly on aid workers from those same foreign countries and put them in danger.[16]

Even before the invasion in March 2003, the United States had put humanitarian aid organizations in a difficult position. Deploying military jargon from his previous career as an army general and commander of the Joint Chiefs of Staff, then Secretary of State Colin Powell saluted American aid organizations in 2001 as 'a force multiplier for us, such an important part of our combat team'. That the aid organizations then became targets of the armed opponents of the United States is perhaps not so surprising. During more than six months preceding the invasion of Iraq, nongovernmental organizations had consulted with US military officials on a weekly basis, to help plan for the humanitarian crisis that the war would unleash. In January 2003, the Pentagon established the Office of Reconstruction and Humanitarian Assistance, designed to coordinate aid efforts with the State Department; the United States Agency for International Development (USAID); and the Office of US Foreign Disaster Assistance.[17] In May 2003, Andrew Natsios, then USAID administrator, referred to the nongovernmental aid organizations as 'an arm of the government', and criticized them for not acknowledging how much of their funding was provided by the United States.[18]

The 'humanitarian' wars of the post-Cold War years put aid organizations in a bind – a 'damned if you do, damned if you don't' situation. In de Torrenté's view, 'the neutral and impartial nature of humanitarian aid is undermined' both 'when an organization agrees to cooperate with a belligerent' and when it 'opposes a war because it will generate victims'.[19] Not every humanitarian organization followed such a strict notion of impartiality. The different ways humanitarian organizations (such as the ICRC) and human rights organizations (such as Human Rights Watch) conceptualized impartiality contributed to the disagreements between them.[20] Julie Mertus reports the positions that various organizations took during the debates over humanitarian intervention starting in the early 1990s. Amnesty International maintained that human rights groups 'should not involve themselves in debates about military interventions, because these are primarily political questions that are properly in the domain of governments and the United Nations'. Human Rights Watch, by contrast, made decisions on a case-by-case basis, 'considering the scale of abuses, whether nonmilitary means have been exhausted, and whether the intervention is likely to do more good than harm'. Using these criteria, the organization advocated military intervention in Somalia, Bosnia, and Rwanda, but opposed NATO's war over Kosovo. Other similar groups made different judgments, as when Physicians for Human Rights pressed for intervention in Kosovo, including the introduction of ground forces.[21]

A further consideration regarding the impartiality of aid organizations is that the success of a humanitarian intervention typically depends on the extent of post-war economic reconstruction. In the case of Iraq, some observers have suggested that the United States might redeem itself for the dubious legality of launching the war – failure to fulfill the *ius ad bellum* criterion of self-defense, for example – by the successful achievement of post-war political and economic reconstruction: a *ius post bellum*.[22] Perhaps with such a goal in mind, the US Army's First Cavalry Division launched 'Operation Adam Smith', which President Bush described as 'setting up local chambers of commerce, providing Iraqi entrepreneurs with small business loans, and teaching them important skills like accounting, marketing and writing business plans'.[23] It is ironic that, at the same time as we see traditional military support functions undertaken by private corporations, these kinds of civilian tasks are performed by soldiers.[24] Worse than ironic, critics argue, such practices increase the threat to civilian aid workers who are trying to engage in reconstruction in a neutral fashion. The projects pose a potential threat to the soldiers as well, who may be distracted from attending to matters of security, including their own. In this sense, the Bush administration contributed to an erosion of the barrier between combatant and noncombatant.

It is not only the nature of the 'new wars' of the post-Cold War era that poses ethical dilemmas for nongovernmental aid organizations. Their own ambition to play an increasing role in humanitarian relief and reconstruction is also at issue. Thomas Weiss identifies 'a shift from emergency relief to attacking root causes and post-conflict peacebuilding'. Under this 'more ambitious agenda', argues Weiss, 'many humanitarians now aspire to attack the structural conditions that endanger vulnerable populations'. They 'desire to spread development, democracy, human rights and create stable, effective, and legitimate states'. To pursue this broader agenda, the humanitarian groups have sought and obtained increased funding. As Weiss reports, the first decade following the end of the Cold War saw a fivefold increase in the annual resources available to international and nongovernmental aid organizations, from $800 million in 1989 to $4.4 billion in 1999. By 2004 the figure was $10 billion.[25]

The expanded agenda and broader role for the organizations have contributed to undermining their inviolability. As Kenneth Anderson argues,

> as humanitarian action extends increasingly across a range of activities – from crisis relief to post-conflict reconstruction – the justification for humanitarian inviolability appears difficult to sustain by analogy to the ideal of purely neutral humanitarian relief that takes no sides on social or political questions. Nation building and the reconstruction of a society are politically laden, distinctly non-neutral activities that, although closely associated in the field with humanitarian relief, do not operate from the same conceptual basis of neutrality and, hence, inviolability.

Anderson, while regretting the personal losses that members of the United Nations agencies and nongovernmental aid organizations have suffered in Iraq, has little sympathy for their criticism of the United States. They 'cannot have it both ways in Iraq – committed to values and yet neutral – as suits their purpose for that moment'. He accuses the critics of 'willful self-deception, a malicious confusion that is not shared by the Iraqi terrorists who exploit it to sow injury and destruction and death, all with utter political clarity'. Humanitarian aid organizations, if they want to be involved in reconstruction efforts, must support the US agenda for Iraq, he suggests, or else 'doom themselves to irrelevance'.[26]

Yet resistance to the US agenda is likely to persist. Indeed, within the international aid community, suspicion concerning the intentions of the US extends beyond concerns about the war on terror and its corollary program of preventive wars and regime change. In August 2007, for example, one of the world's largest charities, CARE International, announced that it would reject $45 million in US government funding in the form of food aid. The US practice of heavily subsidizing its own agribusiness and shipping interests to provide food for

CARE to sell on African markets actually harmed local farmers by undercutting their prices. 'If someone wants to help you, they shouldn't do it by destroying the very thing that they're trying to promote,' said George Odo, a CARE official who observed the practice in Kenya. 'What's happened to humanitarian organizations over the years is that a lot of us have become contractors on behalf of the government,' he said, echoing sentiments of many aid workers. 'It compromised our ability to speak up when things went wrong.'[27]

Privatization of Security and Lack of Accountability

More disturbing, from a legal and ethical standpoint, than aid organizations acting as contractors for governments are private security organizations. Mercenary armies have been a feature of international conflict for centuries and have played an active role in internal conflicts in Africa, in particular during the twentieth century, despite several international conventions intended to eliminate them.[28] Now they have spread throughout the world and, in the form of private military corporations, have become part of the American way of waging war. Private military corporations such as Sandline and Executive Outcomes were initially implicated mainly in the 'resource wars' which rendered countries such as Sierra Leone ungovernable. Later, companies such as Blackwater, Dyncorp, and Triple Canopy came to play essential roles in the functioning of the US armed forces and in the protection of US diplomats in dangerous posts, for instance in Iraq.[29] The private military corporations are relevant to our topic of the ethical and legal dimensions of aid operations, because they are widely employed to provide security for governmental organizations that are seeking to accomplish a humanitarian purpose. Even if their main mission is to protect government officials and to provide logistic support to the military, the armed personnel of private companies can put aid workers and local civilians at risk – and with little accountability. After the United States, the next largest army in Iraq during the first years of occupation was the army of private military personnel. As Weiss reported, 'the 20,000–25,000 private soldiers in Iraq in 2006 outnumbered the second largest national contingent, the United Kingdom's, by at least three to one'.[30] If one counts all of the private contractors, armed and unarmed (137,000 in September 2007, according to Pentagon figures), they nearly equaled the number of US soldiers.[31] Two private security firms, CACI International and Titan, were implicated in abuses at the Abu Ghraib prison, where almost half of all interrogators and analysts were CACI employees.[32] Clearly, some private security contractors have committed serious crimes against civilians. What laws, if any, hold them accountable?

There is, in fact, very little law governing private military corporations, and even less that is enforceable. Although it seems straightforward to call a person who engages in armed combat for profit outside of a national army a 'mercenary', the definition of the term in international humanitarian law is quite specific. Consider the terms of Article 47(2) of the First Protocol to the Geneva Conventions (1977), listed in Box 5.1. Each element of the definition must be met in order for one to qualify as a mercenary. Geoffrey Best quotes a 'learned friend' to the effect that 'any mercenary who cannot exclude himself from this definition deserves to be shot – and his lawyer with him!'[33] The same is true for subsequent international conventions, such as the 1989 International Convention against the Recruitment, Use, Financing, and Training of Mercenaries. As P. W. Singer points out, representatives of private military companies do not seem concerned that their employees are at any risk of prosecution under the treaty: 'Industry analysts have found

---

Box 5.1 *Definition of 'mercenary' in international humanitarian law*

1 A mercenary shall not have the right to be a combatant or a prisoner of war.

2 A mercenary is any person who:

  a Is specially recruited locally or abroad in order to fight in an armed conflict;

  b Does, in fact, take a direct part in the hostilities;

  c Is motivated to take part in the hostilities essentially by the desire for private gain and, in fact, is promised, by or on behalf of a Party to the conflict, material compensation substantially in excess of that promised or paid to combatants of similar ranks and functions in the armed forces of that Party;

  d Is neither a national of a Party to the conflict nor a resident of territory controlled by a Party to the conflict;

  e Is not a member of the armed forces of a Party to the conflict; and

  f Has not been sent by a State which is not a Party to the conflict on official duty as a member of its armed forces.

Source Article 47 of the First Protocol to the Geneva Conventions (1977).

---

that the Convention, which lacks any monitoring mechanism, has merely added a number of vague, almost impossible to prove, requirements that *all* must be met before an individual can be termed a mercenary and few consequences thereafter.' In effect, as Singer argues, there is a 'vacuum of law' where private military forces are concerned.[34]

In September 2007, the apparent vacuum became front-page news when the Iraqi government accused employees of Blackwater of murdering Iraqi civilians while ostensibly protecting US diplomats. It was only one of some fifty-six shooting incidents in which Blackwater had been involved during that year, and only the best publicized out of many other egregious examples of the private contractors' reckless disregard for the lives of Iraqi civilians. The data on shootings, for example, exclude the many civilians killed when US convoys, guarded by private contractors, destroyed Iraqi cars and their passengers or ran over pedestrians as the convoys sped along highways, seeking to avoid roadside bombs and snipers.[35] In the wake of the September incident, when Blackwater contractors reportedly killed between eight and twenty civilians, the Iraqi government banned the company from working on Iraqi soil. The US government, in the person of Secretary of State Condoleezza Rice, announced that it would conduct an investigation instead. The State Department, she argued, could not function in Iraq without Blackwater.

It turned out that the Iraqi government did not exercise sovereignty over its territory to the extent that it could enforce its decision to ban Blackwater. During his time as head of the Coalition Provisional Authority in 2004, L. Paul Bremer III had issued an order that exempted all US personnel, including private security employees, from Iraqi law. Nor, before 2007 at least, were they subject to the Uniform Code of Military Justice that governed US military personnel. The Blackwater contractors could have been covered under the Military Extraterritorial Jurisdiction Act of 2000. This act provides that a contractor working for the Department of Defense could be subjected to prosecution under US law for crimes committed on the battlefield. In the case of Iraq, however, Blackwater's contract was with the State Department, which led many observers to believe that the employees were not covered by that law. In fact, a 2005 amendment to the act included in the category of those covered a contractor of 'any other Federal agency, or any provisional authority, to the extent such employment relates to supporting the mission of the Department of Defense overseas'. US courts have not yet had the opportunity to rule on whether US diplomats working for the State Department are considered to be 'supporting the mission of the Department of Defense', thereby making the private security forces who protect the diplomats subject to the law.[36] In practice, however, such private security contractors, who committed crimes in Iraq, behaved as if they were immune to prosecution. The worst punishment they could expect would be to lose their jobs. Contractors accused of killing Iraqi civilians typically were whisked out of the country to the safety of the United States, where not a single one was prosecuted.[37]

Political figures in both the United States and Iraq sought to fill the legal lacuna that allowed the accused criminals to go free. In January 2007, legislators revised the Uniform Code of Military Justice (UCMJ) to allow military jurisdiction '[i]n time of declared war *or a contingency operation*' over persons 'serving with or accompanying an armed force in the field'. The addition of the italicized phrase broadened the applicability of the law beyond the previous restriction to declared wars – of which the United States has fought very few. In the wake of the September 2007 Blackwater incident, Deputy US Secretary of Defense Gordon England issued a directive to senior officers in the Pentagon, reminding them that all Defense Department contractors 'are subject to UCMJ jurisdiction and encouraging them to begin legal proceedings against those that have violated military law'.[38] In the meantime, Iraqi legislators drafted a law to bring private contractors under Iraqi jurisdiction. In response, US Secretary of Defense Robert Gates insisted that the Pentagon 'has sufficient legal authority to control its contractors'.[39]

Gates' view lends support to the position of James Cockayne, who – contra Peter Singer – argues that the legal status of what he calls military entrepreneurialism is 'not so much a "vacuum" as a "patchwork" of international regulation that leaves states free to harness private military companies in a manner that renders them free agents within – but very much of – the state system'.[40] The editors of the *International Review of the Red Cross* state unequivocally that 'private military and security companies do not operate in a legal vacuum', yet they acknowledge that the phenomenon of military entrepreneurialism complicates the operation of international humanitarian law: 'The cardinal principle of distinction between persons participating in hostilities and those who are not is, in practice, stretched to its limits when interpreting the multiplicity of possible actions that private military personnel might take in situations of armed conflict.'[41]

Given their problematic legal status, why did the United States continue to employ private military companies in Iraq? As the *New York Times* indicated in its coverage of the September 2007 incidents, 'many American officials now share the view that Blackwater's behavior is increasingly stoking resentment among Iraqis and is proving counterproductive to American efforts to gain support for its military efforts in Iraq'. The paper suggested that 'Blackwater enjoys an unusually close relationship with the Bush administration, and with the State Department and Pentagon in particular'. Between 2002 and 2007 it had received more than a billion dollars in government contracts. Many observers attribute the firm's success to the political connections of Erik Prince, the former soldier who founded Blackwater. He and his wealthy Michigan family donated more than $325,000 to political causes between 1997 and 2007, mainly in support of the Republican Party. In a pattern common for firms in the military–industrial sector, Prince hired prominent government officials to improve his company's access to further contracts. Blackwater employed as its chief operating officer Joseph E. Schmitz, a former inspector general at the Pentagon. Cofer Black, the former chief of counter-terrorism at the CIA, joined Blackwater from the Bush administration after failing to capture Osama bin Laden and put his head on a stick, as we heard him vow to do in Chapter 3.[42]

Another potential reason why the US government maintains reliance on private security firms such as Blackwater is to reduce the risk that its foreign and security policy become too democratic. In the absence of soldiers-for-hire, the government would have to recruit more genuine soldiers, limiting its flexibility to engage in wars and illegal covert activities. With more soldiers under arms and in harm's way, the argument goes, more soldiers' families would scrutinize the rationale for US military involvement. Moreover, regular soldiers would be more reluctant than the private contractors to violate the law or fundamental moral principles. Colonel David Hackworth, a highly decorated veteran of the Vietnam War made a similar argument in October 2002, even before the invasion of Iraq: 'These new mercenaries work for the Defense and State Department and Congress looks the other way,' he explained. 'It's a very dangerous situation. It allows us to get into fights where we would be reluctant to send the Defense Department or the CIA. The American taxpayer is paying for our own mercenary army, which violates what our founding fathers said.'[43] There is a certain logic to Hackworth's contention. By the end of 2007, more than a thousand employees of military corporations had been killed in Iraq. If they had been soldiers rather than private subcontractors, that number would have represented a 25 percent increase in combat deaths of US military personnel in the Iraq War to that point – an increase that could be politically consequential.

Another form of 'subcontracting' raised some of the same ethical and legal problems as private military troops did. It entailed the use of local forces to help defeat the designated enemies in humanitarian and anti-terror wars – a practice redolent of the era of European colonial expansion. The United States, for example, supported the armed militia forces of the Kosovo Liberation Army (KLA) to expel Serb forces from the province in 1999. In effect, NATO acted as the KLA's air force. The US adopted a similar approach in Afghanistan, starting from October 2001. As the US air forces bombed Taliban and al Qaeda positions, US Army Special Forces infiltrated the country and recruited the militia forces of the Northern Alliance to carry out major ground operations. In the course of the 'surge', intended to stabilize the security situation in Iraq during 2007, US military units forged alliances of convenience with various Sunni tribal leaders to wage battle against forces that the US government called al Qaeda in Iraq.

Making common cause with indigenous forces provided obvious benefits to the United States in limiting the numbers of US soldiers put in harm's way and in saving money. Yet it posed numerous problems. Some were of a practical nature, when the indigenous forces were unwilling or unable to carry out the necessary tasks. For example, local forces are evidently partly to blame for allowing Osama bin Laden to escape from the Tora Bora cave complex on the border with Pakistan. Sometimes reliance on such forces exacerbated a given situation. In Kosovo during 1998, for example, the KLA provoked the Serb authorities by carrying out attacks against Serb police forces and civilians. Serb retaliation against Kosovar Albanian civilians brought increased sympathy for the Albanian cause and helped induce NATO intervention. The KLA, whose ranks included mafia criminals and terrorists, exerted a baneful influence on post-war Kosovo, complicating prospects for peaceful reconstruction and accommodation with Belgrade and the local Serb population.

From an ethical and legal standpoint, the main issues that implicate the subcontracting of local forces are crimes against noncombatants. The same logic that led the United States to declare that the fighters of the Taliban and al Qaeda were not privileged belligerents under the Geneva Conventions applies as well to the irregular forces of Afghani or Iraqi tribes. As non-state actors, these were not parties to the laws of war and they did not observe them. Among the better-known instances of violations was the murder of prisoners captured by the Northern Alliance, when they suffocated in a sealed truck ostensibly taking them to prison. Some actions of the Afghan mercenaries had long-term implications for which the United States bears much responsibility. In subcontracting the hunt for al Qaeda fighters, for example, the United States offered substantial bounties to anyone who would turn in terrorists to the US authorities. As we have seen in Chapter 3, the promise of monetary reward led some Afghans to denounce neighbors and strangers, many of whom ended up imprisoned for years at Guantánamo and elsewhere.

Some proponents of humanitarian military interventions would be willing to countenance the negative features of sub-contracting to local armed gangs and private military corporations if it would help save populations at risk. We have seen already how the KLA contributed to ending the Belgrade-sanctioned oppression of Kosovar Albanians. In an earlier period of the wars in former Yugoslavia, a private corporation played a role in training and supporting the Croatian forces in the Krajina, a Serb-dominated region from which Croats had been expelled, in a campaign of ethnic cleansing. The military success of the Croatian units, trained by MPRI – formerly known as Military Professionals Resources Inc., a company whose ranks boasted many prominent former US generals – put pressure on the regime of Slobodan Milošević to agree to the Dayton Accords which ended the war. Yet, much as the KLA contributed to the violent expulsion of the Serbs from Kosovo, the Croatian forces engaged in their own ethnic cleansing, driving some 100,000 Serbs from the region and bringing many indictments for war crimes from the international tribunal for former Yugoslavia. Elsewhere, private corporations became involved in the drug and sex-slave trades. In Bosnia, for example, employees of DynCorp operated a prostitution ring that relied on enslaving young women by confiscating their passports.[44] Employees of the private firms rarely faced legal sanction for any of their crimes. If the overall purpose of subcontracting to armed groups or private security companies is a humanitarian one, the costs to local civilians should certainly be taken seriously.

Humanitarian Bombing

Similar considerations come into play regarding the strategies that humanitarian wars entail. Nongovernmental aid organizations have found it difficult to decide whether or not to endorse military action in support of humanitarian goals, because of the additional human suffering that war itself causes. Moreover, some methods of warfare are less discriminate than others and put civilians at considerable risk. The practice of aerial bombardment lies at the core of US military strategy: it is the legacy of the strategic bombing campaigns of World War II and reflects the remarkable advances in technology since then. Calling for international military action in support of humanitarian goals typically means asking the United States to bomb.

During the conflict in former Yugoslavia, when Bosnia was ravaged by Serb militia forces and its capital Sarajevo was under siege, some humanitarian organizations urged the United States and its European allies to defend Bosnian civilians with military force. At the time, rump Yugoslavia (Serbia and Montenegro) and its former constituent republics were under a UN-imposed arms embargo, originally intended to damp down the conflict. Critics pointed out, however, that the embargo favored Serbia, which controlled much of the arsenal of the Yugoslav People's Army and whose troops were occupying the weapons-production facilities in Bosnia. Some supporters of besieged Bosnia began to adopt the slogan 'Lift and strike', urging a lifting of the arms embargo so that the

Bosnian government forces could arm themselves, defend the country and help the intervention by US and NATO air forces to strike Serb artillery positions in the hills surrounding the capital. The campaign by and large failed. The western military response to the mass atrocities carried out in Bosnia came too late to save many civilians, but eventually western pressure (and the US-backed Croatian military offensive in the Krajina) contributed to Slobodan Milošević's decision to sign on to the Dayton Accords.

The wars of Yugoslav succession did not end at Dayton, however – not least because the accords failed to address the situation in Kosovo. The largely nonviolent resistance to Serb control yielded to military action, as the KLA entered the fray and armed Serb units carried out reprisals to terrorize and expel Kosovar Albanian civilians. Calls for foreign intervention led to the NATO air war of March 1999. US leaders expected that a short bombing campaign would bring Milošević to the negotiating table, but instead the war lasted for seventy-eight days. The air war against Serbia highlighted aspects of US military strategy which had become evident already in the 1991 Gulf War – in particular, the targeting of so-called dual-use facilities such as electric grids, transportation networks, sewage and water stations, and the like. International humanitarian law provides constraints on disproportionate damage to civilian life and property during actual combat. But it is largely silent on the long-term impact of destruction of dual-use targets of this kind. Bombing of these facilities may cause few civilian deaths at first, but in time many people die from infection and disease through lack of access to clean water, electricity, or modern medical care. Scholars and activists have argued that this lacuna in the law should be filled with meaningful prohibitions.[45]

Even groups that in some cases supported the use of US military force for humanitarian purposes still sought to play a role in limiting the damage to civilians resulting from those wars. Human Rights Watch, for example, issued regular reports on the military practices of major countries that relied heavily on bombing. This organization monitored the US wars in Iraq in 1991, in Kosovo in 1999, and in Afghanistan and Iraq more recently, as well as the decade of Russian military involvement in Chechnya.[46] It regularly reminds the relevant states of their obligations under international humanitarian law, and even points out which practices tend to cause the most violations – such as indiscriminate use of ground-launched cluster bombs in heavily populated areas, or, during the March 2003 invasion of Iraq, attacks intended to kill top Iraqi leaders by tracing signals from their satellite telephones. The success rate in the latter case was evidently 0 for 50, with many civilians killed unintentionally.[47] There is some evidence that a few countries limited their use of cluster bombs in response to such criticism, but the overall impact of nongovernmental organizations on state military practice is still unclear.[48] Human Rights Watch also issued reports that criticized the practices of the weaker side in these conflicts, for instance the Chechen separatists and Saddam Hussein's army, and especially the use of so-called human shields; but presumably the criticism had even less effect there than on the behavior of the major powers.[49] Dictatorships and armed rebel groups are not likely to act in accordance with international public opinion or with the views of their own domestic constituencies – the way the governments of democracies are expected to do.[50]

This chapter has suggested that the democracies' record of protecting civilians, even in ostensibly humanitarian operations, leaves much to be desired. Many democracies – most prominently, but not exclusively, the United States – express the ideological conviction that their system is the best one for promoting human rights and security. The expansion of the

European Union into the former Soviet bloc, for example, was premised on such a conviction. Not surprisingly, members of nongovernmental humanitarian organizations – many of whom come from North America and Europe – share the values underlying such convictions. When those shared values lead to support for policies of 'regime change', or even to externally driven programs for reconciliation and reconstruction in post-conflict zones, they come into conflict with other values considered central to the project of humanitarianism: neutrality, impartiality, inviolability. Under these circumstances, the opponents of military occupations in the service of regime change and the 'spoilers' of post-conflict settlements become tainted with the epithet 'terrorists', and they often act accordingly, deliberately targeting the personnel of international organizations and aid groups. In response, nongovernmental organizations may come to depend increasingly on governments for their protection, and governments, to rely increasingly on private corporations. In this new world, ethical dilemmas compound legal uncertainty. What in the 1990s appeared as part of a progressive agenda based on the 'responsibility to protect' threatens to evolve in the new century into a mere sideshow of the war on terror.

Conclusion

In the years before the attacks of 11 September 2001, when the US reaction had not yet forced terrorism to the top of the international agenda, the community of states and nongovernmental organizations had arguably achieved considerable success in promoting limitations on weapons and warfare and in advancing the cause of human rights worldwide. Perhaps one should not be surprised that the influence of a nascent 'global civil society', whose very existence some observers doubt, would prove no match for that of the United States, the greatest military power the world has ever known. When US officials vowed to 'take off the shackles', to use 'any means at our disposal', and to work on 'the dark side', one might have expected the worst. As this book has described, things got pretty bad.

Chapter 1 provided a framework for thinking about the impact of norm entrepreneurs who sought to improve human rights and security in the years following the Cold War. Activists, government officials, and others working in the field of human rights and international humanitarian law sought to expand the scope of protections available to civilians caught up in war. During the 1990s they seemed to be making considerable progress, with initiatives such as the Ottawa Mine Ban Treaty of 1997, the International Criminal Court, established by the Rome Statute of 1998, and the emerging consensus that the International Committee of the Red Cross claimed to find for granting customary law status to norms intended to protect civilians. The war on terror called into question this picture of steady progress. At best, we observed something like two steps forward, one step back.

Chapter 2 attributed part of the problem to controversies over definitions of terrorism. The standard aphorism that one state's terrorist is another's freedom fighter captures only one dimension. Questions remain about whether killing government officials and military personnel constitutes terrorism and whether it is useful to speak of 'state terrorism' when government officials and military personnel kill innocent civilians for political purposes. And what about when they kill innocent civilians for military purposes, as in the aerial bombardment of population centers (a practice not coincidentally called 'terror-bombing' during World War II)? The chapter that summarized an emerging view that highlights the distinction between laws criminalizing terrorism carried out by non-state actors and existing laws covering war crimes and human rights abuses – particularly, international humanitarian law and instruments such as the Genocide Convention and the Torture Convention. States will stand a better chance of eradicating political violence and terrorism if they adhere to the laws of war and to human rights standards in their own behavior.

States risk violating those standards in their treatment of suspected terrorists, as Chapter 3 explained. First, the law itself is unclear in many respects about what rights unlawful belligerents should enjoy and about the way to understand concepts such as direct participation in hostilities, which may determine whether 'enemy combatants' can be targeted for long-distance killing. Second, even when the law is clear – as in the prohibition of torture – that is no guarantee that states will follow it. There is a grave risk that the United States' flouting of domestic and international bans on torture will be taken as a precedent for other states to follow suit. There is strong evidence, for example, that the US program of extraordinary rendition – kidnapping suspects and sending them to countries

where they face torture – did, in effect, reintroduce the practice
of torture to places, such as Morocco, which were making good
progress towards limiting it.[1]

Chapter 4 described the paradoxical possibility that, despite
the widespread global opposition to the US war against Iraq,
the norm of preventive action against terrorism may be spread-
ing through the international system. Given the disastrous
results of the Iraq War, such a development would have dangerous consequences for human rights. The chapter suggested that there may be some hope that 'preventive action'
will be defined broadly enough to render military force a
matter of last resort – a policy very different from the one the
Bush administration pursued. The 'high-level panel' of leading
specialists in foreign and security policy which convened at the
request of the UN Secretary General endorsed a rather expansive conception of prevention when it issued its report in
2004: 'Preventing mass-casualty terrorism requires a deep
engagement to strengthen collective security systems, amelio-
rate poverty, combat extremism, end the grievances that flow
from war, tackle the spread of infectious disease and fight
organized crime.'[2]

The high-level panel's agenda sounds reasonable enough.
But what if countries fail in implementing it? A 'failed state' is
often defined as the opposite of a country that fulfills all of the
tasks considered necessary to prevent terrorism. When such
states descend into civil war, suffer widespread famine or disease, or become havens for terrorists, they are likely to find
themselves targets for outside intervention, in keeping with
the widely endorsed Responsibility to Protect mandate or
as a preventive or punitive anti-terror measure. Chapter 5
addressed the problems that humanitarian aid groups face in
such situations. Their traditional attributes of neutrality,
impartiality, and inviolability become difficult for them to
maintain and for others to respect. As they come under threat

from hostile armed groups, they may be tempted to seek security from the governments of the intervening states and from the private security contractors upon whom those governments depend. Those private security forces inhabit a nearly lawless zone; they are mercenaries in every sense except the formal legal one. Their contributions to humanitarian operations are on balance negative, as are the aerial bombardment campaigns in support of humanitarian intervention, also treated in this chapter. Both end up harming the civilians they are supposed to protect.

Overall, this picture of our world in the midst of the Global War on Terror is a bleak one. Yet it coincides with the impressions of other scholars, coming from different backgrounds and addressing a somewhat different set of questions. Kim Lane Scheppele, for example, has studied the process by which legal practices come to be adopted in countries throughout the world. She calls it 'public law globalization'. Scheppele's understanding of what she designates as the first wave of public law globalization – regarding international human rights – is similar to what we considered in the first chapter as progress in the stigmatization and punishment of torture and other human rights abuses. In this sense, Scheppele's first wave encompasses what Ellen Lutz and Kathryn Sikkink call the 'justice cascade'. Scheppele writes that it

> is now being countered by a second wave of public law globalization. Since 9/11, the UN Security Council and regional bodies have quickly developed international security law to create an international web of mechanisms for battling terrorism. But international security law, unlike international human rights law, has teeth. Given the UN Security Council's powers to sanction non-complying countries, international security law is immediately a more serious business than the international human rights monitoring system, which relies

primarily on naming and shaming without the associated sanctioning power. International security law can be mandated by the Security Council in a manner not available to the human rights community.

Scheppele points out that the new laws adopted in the wake of 9/11 'have constitutional implications – centralizing power in the hands of executives within systems of otherwise divided government, increasing ease of surveillance of publics, truncating due process guarantees, changing the role of the military in civic life, and restricting individual rights of liberty, speech, association and privacy'. In the days and weeks following the 9/11 attacks, the UN Security Council passed Resolution 1368, calling the attacks 'a threat to international peace and security', and Resolution 1373, which Scheppele describes as 'a far-reaching and essentially legislative resolution that, for the first time in the Security Council's history, used binding authority under Chapter VII of the UN Charter to require all member states to change their domestic laws in very specific ways' or face sanctions.[3]

The Security Council established a Counter-Terrorism Committee mandated to monitor the implementation of Resolution 1373. Jeremy Greenstock, its first chair, insisted that 'monitoring performance against other international conventions, including human rights law, is outside the scope of the Counter-Terrorism Committee's mandate' and conveys, in Scheppele's assessment, a clear preference for security measures and a lack of regard for their implications for human rights. His views contrast sharply with those of Mary Robinson, then UN High Commissioner for Human Rights. As we have seen in Chapter 2, she maintained that 'ensuring that innocent people do not become the victims of counter-terrorism measures should always be an important component of any antiterrorism strategy'.[4] Which view prevails will determine the extent to which practices in the war on terror overwhelm the human rights protections established over decades, and – if one thinks of habeas corpus – even over centuries.

To pose the question whether state practice in the war on terror will trump the evolution of norms to protect human rights is somewhat misleading, however. For one thing, not all states follow the same practices. Scheppele's research, for example, indicates that different types of states reacted to the Security Council's program for counter-terrorism in different ways. Some were more intent on preserving their constitutional prerogatives than others. This is similar to the range of responses that states have taken to the expansion of the preventive motive for military action under the guise of 'preemption', as discussed in Chapter 4. The broader the notion of 'prevention', the less likely military force will be the first resort.

Despite the preponderant military position of the United States in the international system, the shape of future international law – even for those who see state practice as providing the main source of law – does not depend on one state alone. Much hinges on how other states react to US departures from traditional norms, such as prohibitions against preventive wars, assassination, or torture. In many of these cases, the jury is still out or the verdict is ambiguous. Regarding extraordinary renditions, for instance, some European countries' security services, if not the governments themselves, apparently cooperated with the CIA to kidnap suspects. Yet, when the news leaked, there was considerable outrage and efforts to bring the responsible parties to account. In Italy, for example, prosecutors indicted Niccolò Pollari, former head of the security service, along with twenty-six US citizens suspected of being CIA agents, for the abduction of Egyptian cleric Hassan Mustafa Osama Nasr off the streets of Milan in February 2003. Abu Omar, as he was also known, smuggled a letter out of Egypt, where, he claimed, he had been tortured.[5] If Italian prosecutors managed to convict Pollari and the other Italian and US agents (*in absentia*, because they had all fled the country), that would serve as some kind of repudiation of the illegal practice of extraordinary rendition. Likewise, the strong position taken by the Council of Europe against the renditions and the use of secret prisons, if backed by further actions and statements by the member countries, could have a stigmatizing effect on the practices.[6]

The investigation of Donald Rumsfeld and others by a German court, discussed in Chapters 1 and 3, provides an example of particularly ambiguous behavior, which makes it difficult to predict whether the US norm of torturing terror suspects will be endorsed or repudiated by the society of states. In this case, the German prosecutor deferred to the US district court, which excused Rumsfeld's behavior as, in effect, torture in the line of duty.

We have queried the notion of 'state practice', given the range of possible state responses to heretofore illegal action rehabilitated in the interest of the war on terror. Prevailing views on customary law would suggest that a preponderance of states would have to support, or acquiesce in, the new understanding in order for it to attain legal status. In a similar fashion, we might consider whether it makes sense to accept that the state practice of, say, the United States should be decided by a narrow circle of political appointees in the Pentagon, when large numbers of professional military officers and lawyers opposed their violations of existing law and custom. Considerable evidence indicates great unease within the ranks, especially of the military legal experts – the so-called Judge Advocates General or JAGs. Many JAGs objected to the Bush administration's Military Commissions Act of 2006, for example, preferring that the United States abide by Common Article 3 of the Geneva Conventions which, as the Supreme Court also indicated, requires 'a regularly constituted court affording all the judicial guarantees which are recognized as indispensable by civilized peoples'. According to the *New York Times*, Donald J. Guter, a retired admiral and the US Navy's top uniformed lawyer, 'said it would be a mistake for Congress to try to undo the Supreme Court ruling'. Yet he and his fellow JAGs 'after objecting to the planned military commissions found their advice pointedly unheeded'. 'This was the concern all along of the JAGs', Admiral Guter said. 'It's a matter of defending what we always thought was the rule of law and proper behavior for civilized nations.'[7]

Disgruntled military professionals and civil servants expressed their opposition to the Bush administration's lawlessness in various ways. Some of them, presumably, were the sources of the leaks that allowed journalists such as Mark Danner, Seymour Hersh, and Jane Mayer to put together the history of the crimes of the Bush administration. Others fought within their organizations to return to the rule of law. Still others cooperated with 'transnational norm entrepreneurs' to try to maintain basic protections such as habeas corpus – with inconclusive results so far.[8] Their efforts provide some hope that democracies will manage to preserve the freedoms that the terrorists are supposed to want to destroy, even while those freedoms are under attack by our own governments.

I began this book by posing a distinction, somewhat artificial, but I thought still useful, between the understanding of the laws of war by military professionals and by human rights activists and lawyers. I suggested that the phrase 'law of armed conflict', favored by the former, implied different priorities from 'international humanitarian law', favored by the latter. Kenneth Anderson, writing in 1998, seemed to suggest something similar. He appears in retrospect to have been in the process of moving from a position on the laws of war which was close to that of the human rights community towards one that rather resembled the views of thoughtful military lawyers

and officers. He still used the phrase 'international humanitarian law', for example, although his remarks expound upon a
military point of view and reflect the distinction I have highlighted:

> International humanitarian law seeks to create a culture,
> indeed a cult, of war, one most peculiar in the history of cul-
> ture, because it is transnational and not located in a specific
> geography, grounded instead in the sense of a shared profes-
> sion, among men-at-arms, and, in war-time, only too fre-
> quently contrary to immediate human interest . . . [I]n the
> end, the culture relevant to respect for international humani-
> tarian law is not the culture of legality and the cult of lawyers,
> but instead it is the culture of the professional honour of sol-
> diers and what they are willing or not willing to do on the bat-
> tlefield.[9]

Or, he might add, if he were writing after 9/11, what they are
willing or not willing to do in prisons, secret detention camps,
and interrogation chambers. The bright spot in the otherwise
dark picture I have painted in this book is the role that some
military officers and soldiers have played in resisting the
degradation of their profession that came with the Bush
administration's arrogant dismissal of the value of the laws
of war. The military lawyers who raised concerns with the
American Bar Association, the Pentagon officials who leaked
the 'torture memos' to the press, the whistle-blowers at Abu
Ghraib and elsewhere were acting in defense of their professional honor, as Anderson described it.

When administration officials argued that al Qaeda and
Taliban prisoners were entitled to no protections under the
Geneva Conventions, they pointed out, plausibly, that US soldiers captured by those organizations would be unlikely to
receive such protections. Therefore the expectation of reciprocity that undergirds much of international law would be
absent. When presented with such arguments, many military

lawyers and officers respond with something to the effect that 'we don't want our American soldiers to be mistreated if they are taken prisoner'. Did they fail to understand the argument about reciprocity? I doubt it. I think they had become so thoroughly socialized to the norm of humane treatment of prisoners that they were unwilling to abandon it just because a gang of terrorists refused to respect it. My sense is that they had a more profound understanding of how norms work than their political superiors did. They understood that the occasional exception, if properly stigmatized, could actually serve to bolster the norm, whereas if the exception becomes the rule, all bets are off.

We may not share Anderson's confidence that the culture of military honor will be enough to prevent our descent into barbarism, even in the absence of responsible moral leadership. But we should find some hope in the common decency of professional soldiers and officers. At the same time, however, we cannot expect them to maintain that basic decency as they face the pressures of fighting long wars of occupation against hostile populations in Iraq, Afghanistan and elsewhere. They may not succeed in halting the US administration's efforts to make 'worst practice' the basis of future international law, but they deserve credit for trying.

Notes

INTRODUCTION

1 Julian Glover, 'British believe Bush is more dangerous than Kim Jong-Il', *Guardian*, 3 November 2006.
2 David Wippman, 'Introduction: Do new wars call for new laws?', in David Wippman and Matthew Evangelista, eds, *New Wars, New Laws? Applying the Laws of War in 21st Century Conflicts* (Ardsley, NY: Transnational Publishers, 2005), ch. 1.
3 I argued that under certain conditions such organizations could be influential even in security policy: Matthew Evangelista, *Unarmed Forces: The Transnational Movement to End the Cold War* (Ithaca, NY: Cornell University Press, 1999). For a thoughtful assessment of whether the 'international community' serves as a counterweight to the influence of the United States in shaping international law, see Michael Byers and Georg Nolte, eds, *United States Hegemony and the Foundations of International Law* (Cambridge, UK: Cambridge University Press, 2003).
4 Particularly influential on my thinking have been: Harold Hongju Koh, 'Why do nations obey international law?', *The Yale Law Journal*, vol. 106, no. 8 (June 1997); id., 'The 1998 Frankel Lecture: Bringing international law home', *Houston Law Review*, vol. 35 (Fall 1998); Richard Price, 'Emerging norms and anti-personnel landmines', in Christian Reus-Smit, ed., *The Politics of International Law* (Cambridge, UK: Cambridge University Press, 2004), ch. 5; Michael Byers, *Custom, Power and the Power of Rules: International Relations and Customary International Law* (New York: Cambridge University Press, 1999); Nicholas J. Wheeler, *Saving Strangers: Humanitarian Intervention in International Society* (Oxford, UK: Oxford University Press, 2000); Neta Crawford, *Argument and Change in World Politics: Ethics, Decolonization, and Humanitarian Intervention* (Cambridge, UK: Cambridge University Press, 2002).

5 Matthew Evangelista, *The Chechen Wars: Will Russia Go the Way of the Soviet Union?* (Washington, DC: Brookings Institution, 2002).
6 See in particular the book with that title, Kim Lane Scheppele, *The International State of Emergency* (forthcoming).
7 *The Defense Monitor*, vol. 36, no. 6 (November/December 2007), p. 7.

CHAPTER 1 NORMS VERSUS PRACTICE IN INTERNATIONAL LAW AND ETHICS

1 An excellent discussion of these issues is found in Michael Byers, *War Law: International Law and Armed Conflict* (London: Atlantic Books, 2005). On just war theory, see Mona Fixdal and Dan Smith, 'Humanitarian intervention and just war', *Mershon International Studies Review*, vol. 42 (1998).
2 US Army, *The Law of Land Warfare*, FM 27–10, Department of the Army Field Manual, 1956, rev. 1976, para. 41.
3 E. H. Carr, *The Twenty Years' Crisis, 1919–1939: An Introduction to the Study of International Relations*, 2nd edn (New York: Harper and Row, 1946 (original publication 1939, paperback edn 1964), p. 173.
4 Kenneth Anderson, 'Who owns the rules of war? The war in Iraq demands a rethinking of the international rules of conduct', *New York Times Magazine*, 13 April 2003; 'The role of the United States military lawyer in projecting a vision of the laws of war', *Chicago Journal of International Law*, vol. 4, no. 2 (Fall 2003).
5 Robert Kagan, 'Power and weakness', *Policy Review*, n. 113, June 2002.
6 Mark Turner, 'UN panel close to framing a law on state aggression', *Financial Times*, 6 February 2007.
7 On security policy, see Matthew Evangelista, *Unarmed Forces: The Transnational Movement to End the Cold War* (Ithaca, NY: Cornell University Press, 1999). On human rights, Margaret Keck and Kathryn Sikkink, *Activists beyond Borders: Advocacy Networks in International Politics* (Ithaca, NY: Cornell University Press, 1998); and Thomas Risse, Steven Ropp and Kathryn Sikkink, eds, *The Power of Human Rights: International Norms and Domestic Change* (Cambridge, UK: Cambridge University Press, 1999). For an overview of the mechanisms of transnational contention, see

Sidney Tarrow, *The New Transnational Activism* (Cambridge, UK: Cambridge University Press, 2005). The section that follows draws on a draft paper, 'Human rights at war' (August 2007), co-authored with Sidney Tarrow and used with his permission.

8 Don Hubert, 'The landmine ban: A case study in humanitarian advocacy', Occasional Paper #42, Watson Institute, Brown University, 2000; and Richard Price, 'Reversing the gun sights: Transnational civil society targets landmines', *International Organization*, vol. 52, no. 3 (Summer 1998). The most comprehensive study of this issue is Margarita Petrova, *Leadership Competition and the Creation of Norms: A Cross-National Study of Weapons Restrictions*, Cornell University PhD dissertation (January 2007).

9 International Campaign to Ban Landmines, Landmine Monitor Factsheet, 'Status of Implementation of the 1997 Mine Ban Treaty', 21 June 2004, http://www.icbl.org/lm/factsheets/pdf/ implementation_status_june_2004.pdf.

10 The figures are rough estimates based on the annual editions of the *Landmine Monitor Report*, whose reporting categories are, unfortunately, not consistent year to year: http://www.icbl. org/lm/.

11 *Landmine Monitor Report 2006*, http://www.icbl.org/lm/2006/ developments.html.

12 ICBL Statement during the High Level Segment, delivered by Steve Goose, Director of Human Rights Watch Arms Division and Head of ICBL Delegation at Nairobi Summit on a Mine-Free World: First Five-Year Review Conference for the Mine Ban Treaty, 3 December 2004, http://hrw.org/english/docs /2004/12/03/global10236.htm; Human Rights Watch, 'U.S.: New Landmines for Iraq Raise Fears of Civilian Risk', February 2005, http://hrw.org/english/docs/2005/02/28/usint10214.htm.

13 'Military hopes this landmine can keep peace', *New York Daily News*, 13 September 2005; *Landmine Monitor Report 2006*.

14 Scott Stedjan and Matt Schaaf, 'If it looks like a landmine, smells like a landmine. . .' *Foreign Policy in Focus*, 28 August 2006, http://www.fpif.org/fpiftxt/3468. The website for the Project Manager Close Combat Systems, http://ccsweb.pica.army.mil/ about.htm, is particularly informative on the weapons that are of interest to the Pentagon.

15 Carr, *Twenty Years' Crisis* (above, n. 3), p. 79.

16 Richard Price, 'Emerging customary norms and anti-personnel landmines', in Christian Reus-Smit, ed., *The Politics of International Law* (Cambridge, UK: Cambridge University Press, 2004), ch. 5.

17 Jean-Marie Henckaerts and Louise Doswald-Beck, eds, *Customary International Humanitarian Law* (Cambridge, UK: Cambridge University Press, 2005). For a summary, see Jean-Marie Henckaerts, 'Study on customary international humanitarian law: A contribution to the understanding and respect for the rule of law in armed conflict', *International Review of the Red Cross*, vol. 87, no. 857 (March 2005).

18 Michael Byers, *Custom, Power and the Power of Rules: International Relations and Customary International Law* (New York: Cambridge University Press, 1999); Price, 'Emerging customary norms' (above, n. 16).

19 David Cortright, *A Peaceful Superpower: The Movement against War in Iraq* (Goshen, IN: Fourth Freedom, 2004)

20 Ellen Lutz and Kathryn Sikkink, 'The justice cascade: The evolution and impact of foreign human rights trials in Latin America', *Chicago Journal of International Law*, vol. 2, no. 1 (Spring 2001); Kathryn Sikkink and Carrie Booth Walling, 'Errors about trials: The emergence and impact of the justice cascade', paper presented at NYU Law School, 2 April 2007, http://iilj.org/research/documents/Session11.Sikkink.pdf; Chandra Lekha Sriram, *Globalizing Justice for Mass Atrocities: A Revolution in Accountability* (London: Routledge, 2005). For Amnesty International's efforts, see Ann Marie Clark, *Diplomacy of Conscience: Amnesty International and Changing Human Rights Norms* (Princeton, NJ: Princeton University Press, 2001).

21 US Senate Republican Policy Committee, 'Are U.S. interests being disserved by the International Committee of the Red Cross?', 13 June 2005, p. 7.

22 Neil A. Lewis, 'Official attacks top law firms over detainees', *New York Times*, 13 January 2007.

23 Naomi Roht-Arriaza, *The Pinochet Effect: Transnational Justice in the Age of Human Rights* (Philadelphia, PA: University of Pennsylvania Press, 2005), p. 7.

24 Roht-Arriaza, *The Pinochet Effect* (above), p. 56.

25 Sikkink and Carrie Booth Walling, 'Errors about trials' (above, n. 20).

26 Thomas F. Hogan, Chief Judge, United States District Court for the District of Columbia, In Re: Iraq and Afghanistan Detainees Litigation, Memorandum Opinion, 27 March 2007.

27 David Rising, 'Torture probe of US officials rejected', Associated Press, 27 April 2007; on the general issue, Leslie C. Green, 'War crimes, crimes against humanity, and command responsibility', *Naval War College Review*, vol. 50, no. 2 (Spring 1997).

28 Information on the US position is available at the website of the American Nongovernmental Organizations Coalition for the International Criminal Court, http://www.amicc.org/.

29 International Commission on Intervention and State Sovereignty (Gareth Evans and Mohamed Sahnoun, co-chairs), *The Responsibility to Protect* (Ottawa: International Development Research Centre, 2001).

30 Both reports are available at http://www.responsibilitytoprotect.org/index.php/pages/20. For a discussion, see Thomas G. Weiss, *Humanitarian Intervention: Ideas in Action* (Cambridge, UK: Polity, 2007).

31 Secretary Colin L. Powell, Remarks to the National Foreign Policy Conference for Leaders of Nongovernmental Organizations, U.S. Department of State, Washington, DC, 26 October 2001.

CHAPTER 2 TERRORISM: DEFINITIONAL CONTROVERSIES

1 For a thoughtful discussion of these issues, see Thomas Weigend, 'The universal terrorist: The international community grappling with a definition', *Journal of International Criminal Justice*, vol. 4 (November 2006).

2 This discussion draws upon Center for Defense Information, 'A brief history of terrorism', 2 July 2003, http://www.cdi.org/friendlyversion/printversion.cfm?documentID=1502; and David C. Rapoport, 'Fear and trembling: Terrorism in three religious traditions', *American Political Science Review*, vol. 78, no. 3 (September 1984), pp. 668–72.

3 The history of the three groups is reviewed in Mia Bloom, *Dying to Kill: The Allure of Suicide Terror* (New York: Columbia University Press, 2005).

4 The league definition is quoted on a United Nations website, http://www.unodc.org/unodc/terrorism_definitions.html.

5 United States Department of Defense, Office of Joint Chiefs of Staff, *Joint Publication 1–02: Department of Defense Dictionary of Military and Associated Terms* (Washington, DC : United States Department of Defense, 12 April 2001 – As amended through 13 June 2007), p. 540. Online at: http://www.dtic.mil/doctrine/jel/new_pubs/jp1_02.pdf.

6 Naval Reserve Officers Training Corps, Naval Science Laboratory, Lesson 14, 'Terrorism', n.d., https://www.cnet.navy.mil/cnet/nrotc/cig/nsl/LAB-LESSON%2014.doc (accessed 19 August 2007).

7 Office of the Coordinator for Counter-Terrorism, *Patterns of Global Terrorism 2002*, US Department of State Publication 11038 (Washington, DC: State Department, April 2003), p. 13. Online at: http://www.state.gov/documents/organization/20177.pdf. The US legislation is found in Title 22 of the US Code, Section 2656f(d), http://www4.law.cornell.edu/uscode/html/ uscode22/usc_sec_22_00002656----f000-.html. Starting in 2005 with the publication *Country Reports on Terrorism*, the State Department ceased providing a definition, but instead sought to describe various types of terrorist organizations and activities. See US Department of State, *Country Reports on Terrorism 2006* (April 2007), http://www.state.gov/s/ct/rls/crt/2006/.

8 For some examples, see V. G. Kiernan, *Colonial Empires and Armies, 1815–1960* (Stroud, UK: Sutton, 1982); Manfred Boemeke, Roger Chickering, and Stig Förster, eds, *Anticipating Total War: The German and American Experiences, 1871–1914* (New York: Cambridge University Press, 1999); S. B. Spies, *Methods of Barbarism: Roberts and Kitchener and Civilians in the Boer Republics, January 1900–May 1902* (Cape Town: Human and Rousseau, 1977); David Anderson, *Histories of the Hanged: Britain's Dirty War in Kenya and the End of Empire* (New York: Norton, 2005).

9 For a particularly revealing memoir by one of the leading French organizers and justifiers of torture, see Paul Aussaresses, *Services spéciaux: Algérie, 1955–1957* (Paris: Perrin, 2001). For a discussion of counter-terrorist groups, see Alistair Horne, *A Savage War of Peace: Algeria 1954–1962* (New York: Viking Press, 1977), esp. pp. 148, 184.

10 Fourth Geneva Convention, Article 33 (1). See the discussion in Weigend, 'Universal terrorist' (above, n. 1).

11 For a discussion of the law of military occupation in connection with Israel's policies, see Kathleen Cavanaugh, 'Rewriting law: The case of Israel and the occupied territories', in David Wippman and Matthew Evangelista, eds, *New Wars, New Laws? Applying the Laws of War in 21st Century Conflicts* (Ardsley, NY: Transnational Publishers, 2005), ch. 9.

12 Giulio Douhet, *Command of the Air* (*Il dominio dell'aria*, 1921), translated by Dino Ferrari (New York: Coward-McCann, 1942), p. 10.

13 Douhet, *Command of the Air*, discussed and quoted in Michael S. Sherry, *The Rise of American Air Power: The Creation of Armageddon* (New Haven, CT: Yale University Press, 1987), ch. 2.

14 Quotations in this paragraph are all from Robert C. Batchelder, *The Irreversible Decision, 1939–1950* (New York: Macmillan, 1961), pp. 172–3. For more detail, see Tami Davis Biddle, *Rhetoric and Reality in Air Warfare: The Evolution of British and American Ideas about Strategic Bombing, 1914–1945* (Princeton, NJ: Princeton University Press, 2002).

15 Trenchard's report is available online from the British Public Records Office, http://www.nationalarchives.gov.uk/pathways/ firstworldwar/transcripts/aftermath/air_power_iraq.htm (downloaded 8 September 2007). The quotations in this paragraph come from Geoff Simons, *Iraq: From Sumer to Saddam* (London: St Martins Press, 1994), pp. 179–81, as cited in 'How Britain invented terror bombing in 1920s Iraq', http://en.internationalism.org/wr/ 265_terror1920.htm (accessed 8 September 2007). On the use of air power in other colonies, see Kiernan, *Colonial Empires and Armies* (above, n. 8), pp. 194–201.

16 Diary entry of F. Stevenson for 9 March 1934, quoted in Kiernan, *Colonial Empires and Armies*, p. 200. For a general argument about the distinction between civilized and uncivilized in the ethics of colonialism, see Neta C. Crawford, *Argument and Change in World Politics: Ethics, Decolonization, and Humanitarian Intervention* (Cambridge: Cambridge University Press, 2002).

17 Batchelder, *The Irreversible Decision* (above, n. 14), pp. 174–5.

18 Curtis LeMay, 'Oral history' (interview transcript), 1966, quoted by Marilyn Young in a 2006 conference paper, 'Total war', which is in turn cited in Mark Selden, 'A forgotten holocaust: US

bombing strategy, the destruction of Japanese cities and the American way of war from the Pacific war to Iraq', *Japan Focus*, 2 May 2007, http://japanfocus.org/products/details/2414. See also Sven Lindqvist, *A History of Bombing* (New York: Norton, 2003). The 1952 war plan is quoted in Robert A. Pape, *Bombing to Win: Air Power and Coercion in War* (Ithaca, NY: Cornell University Press, 1996), p. 160.

19 Raphael Littauer and Norman Uphoff, eds, *The Air War in Indochina* (Boston, MA: Beacon Press, 1972); Sahr Conway-Lanz, *Collateral Damage: Americans, Noncombatant Immunity, and Atrocity after World War II* (New York: Routledge, 2006), p. 218; Matthew Evangelista, *The Chechen Wars: Will Russia Go the Way of the Soviet Union?* (Washington, DC: Brookings Institution Press, 2002).

20 Thomas Schelling, *Arms and Influence* (New Haven, CT: Yale University Press, 1966), pp. 17–18. For more on the association between terror and war, see Alessandro Colombo, *La guerra ineguale: Pace e violenza nel tramonto della società internazionale* (Bologna: Il Mulino, 2006).

21 Albert Wohlstetter, 'The delicate balance of terror', Rand Corporation publication P-1472, 6 November 1958, revised December 1958, http://www.rand.org/about/history/wohlstetter/P1472/P1472.html. A later version appeared in *Foreign Affairs*, vol. 37, no. 2 (1959).

22 Conway-Lanz, *Collateral Damage* (above, n. 19). For a discussion of US nuclear strategy, see David Alan Rosenberg, 'A smoking radiating ruin at the end of two hours: Documents on American plans for nuclear war with the Soviet Union', *International Security*, vol. 6, no. 3 (Winter 1981–2).

23 Howard Zinn, 'On terror', Letters to the Editor, *New York Times Sunday Book Review*, 19 August 2007. Civilian harm that can be foreseen, given certain military practices (such as bombing), but is not deliberate, may fall under the category that Neta Crawford calls 'systemic'. See her 'Individual and collective moral responsibility for systemic military atrocity', *Journal of Political Philosophy*, vol. 15, no. 2 (2007).

24 Michael Walzer, *Just and Unjust Wars: A Moral Argument with Historical Illustrations* (New York: Basic Books, 1977), ch. 12, pp. 197–200.

25 Aleksandr Melenberg, 'Nravstvennyi terrorist', *Novaia gazeta*, 4
    July 2005, http://2005.novayagazeta.ru/nomer/2005/47n/n47n-
    s44.shtml.
26 John Reuter, *Chechyna's Suicide Bombers: Desperate, Devout, or
    Deceived?* (Washington, DC: American Committee for Peace in
    Chechnya, 2004), p. 5.
27 Weigend, 'Universal terrorist' (above, n. 1), p. 922.
28 See the discussion of assassination in chapter 3 of Ward Thomas,
    The Ethics of Destruction: Norms and Force in International Relations
    (Ithaca, NY: Cornell University Press, 2001); quotation at p. 60.
29 Weigend, 'Universal terrorist' (above, n. 1), makes this point on
    p. 920.
30 International Convention for the Suppression of Acts of Nuclear
    Terrorism, http://untreaty.un.org/English/Terrorism/English
    _18_15.pdf.
31 International Convention for the Suppression of the Financing of
    Terrorism, http://www.un.org/law/cod/finterr.htm.
32 James Risen and Eric Lichtblau, 'Concerns raised on wider spying
    under new law', *New York Times*, 19 August 2007.
33 http://www.un.org/law/terrorism.htm.
34 The United Nations Global Counter-Terrorism Strategy,
    http:// www.un.org/terrorism/strategy-counter-terrorism.html.
35 The quotation from 1992 comes from the UN website,
    http://www.unodc.org/unodc/terrorism_definitions.html.
36 Mary Robinson, UN High Commissioner for Human Rights,
    March 2002, http://www.unhchr.ch/huricane/huricane.nsf/
    view01/858EF20492884DD6C1256B82003E2A38?open
    document.
37 Article 19(2) of the International Convention for the Suppression
    of Terrorist Bombings of 15 December 1997 and Article 4(2) of
    the Nuclear Terrorism Convention.
38 Weigend, 'Universal terrorist' (above, n. 1), p. 923.
39 'Documents linked to Cuban exile Luis Posada highlighted targets
    for terrorism', National Security Archive Update, 3 May 2007,
    http://www.nsarchive.org; ' "Airlines terror plot" disrupted', BBC
    News, 10 August 2006,
    http://news.bbc.co.uk/1/hi/uk/4778575.stm.
40 Department of Justice, United States Attorney Alice H. Martin
    Northern District of Alabama, 'Alabama free militia members
    plead guilty in US district court', 25 June 2007,

http://www.atf.gov/press/2007press/field/062607nash_militiam
embers-guiltyplea.htm.

41 'A look at the forces behind the anti-immigrant movement',
transcript of a radio broadcast, *Democracy Now*, 2 May
2007, http://www.democracynow.org/article.pl?sid=07/05/02/1
427217.

42 US District Court of Oregon, Memorandum Opinion, United
States of America v. Darren Todd Thurston et al., 21 May 2007,
http://cldc.org/pdf/AikenTEmemo.pdf.

43 'Environmentalist jailed for 13 years after ruled a terrorist',
Democracy Now, 24 May 2007, http://www.democracynow.org/
article.pl?sid=07/05/24/142259; 'Environmentalist gets 13 years
in arson fires', *Associated Press*, 24 May 2007.

44 Helene Cooper and Jim Rutenberg, 'U.S. set to declare Iran
guards terrorists', *New York Times*, 15 August 2007; Helene
Cooper, 'Clinton's Iran vote: The fallout', *New York Times*, 14
October 2007.

45 *National Security Strategy of the United States*, available at:
http://www.whitehouse.gov/nsc/nss/2006/nss2006.pdf.

46 George Bush, quoted in Seymour M. Hersh, 'The redirection', *The
New Yorker*, 5 March 2007; 'Report: U.S. sponsoring Kurdish
guerilla attacks inside Iran', transcript of interview with Reese
Erlich, *Democracy Now*, 27 March 2007, http://www.democracy
now.org/article.pl?sid=07/03/27/1356250; Reese Erlich, *The Iran
Agenda: The Real Story of US Policy and the Middle East Crisis*
(Sausalito, CA: PoliPoint Press, 2007).

47 Richard A. Oppel, Jr, 'Foreign fighters in Iraq are tied to allies of
US', *New York Times*, 22 November 2007.

CHAPTER 3 SUSPECTED TERRORISTS AS
PRISONERS AND TARGETS

1 White House Office of the Press Secretary, 'Remarks by the
president after two planes crash into World Trade Center',
http://www.whitehouse.gov/news/releases/2001/09/20010911.h
tml; and 'Press briefing by Attorney General, Secretary of HHS,
Secretary of Transportation, and FEMA Director',
http://www.whitehouse.gov/news/releases/2001/09/20010911–
10.html, both 11 September 2001.

2 White House Office of the Press Secretary, 'Remarks by the president in photo opportunity with the national security team', 12 September 2001, http://www.whitehouse.gov/news/releases/2001/09/20010912–4.html.

3 It was published in *Al Quds Al Arabi*, a London-based newspaper, in August 1996 and is available in English translation at: http://www.pbs.org/newshour/terrorism/international/fatwa_1996.html.

4 *9/11 Commission Report* (New York: W. W. Norton, n.d. (2004)), p. 102.

5 White House Office of the Press Secretary, 'President urges readiness and patience', 15 September 2001, http://www.whitehouse.gov/news/releases/2001/09/20010915–4.html.

6 White House Office of the Press Secretary, 'Remarks by the president upon arrival', http://www.whitehouse.gov/news/releases/2001/09/20010916–2.html, 16 September 2001; White House Office of the Press Secretary, 'Guard and reserves "define spirit of America" ', Remarks by the President to Employees at the Pentagon, 17 September 2001, http://www.whitehouse.gov/news/releases/2001/09/20010917–3.html.

7 Ron Suskind, *The One Percent Doctrine: Deep Inside America's Pursuit of Its Enemies Since 9/11* (New York: Simon and Schuster, 2006), pp. 3, 14–15, 20–1.

8 Quoted in Suskind, *One Percent Doctrine* (above), pp. 17–18.

9 S. J. Resolution 23, Authorization for Use of Military Force, Public Law No: 107–40, 18 September 2001, http://www.yale.edu/lawweb/avalon/sept_11/sjres23_eb.htm.

10 Susskind, *One Percent Doctrine* (above, n. 7), pp. 19–20.

11 Jean-Marie Colombani, 'Nous sommes tous Américains', *Le Monde*, 13 September 2001. Bernard Kouchner claims to have coined the expression first in an article he submitted to the newspaper's editor on the evening of the 11th, but which was not published until the 14th. See " 'Tous Américains": Colombani plagiaire?', http://www.acrimed.org/article1286.html.

12 'USA: Treatment of prisoners in Afghanistan and Guantánamo Bay undermines human rights', 15 April 2002, http://web.amnesty.org/library/index/engamr510542002.

13 Donald Rumsfeld, US Secretary of Defense, 11 January 2002.

14 US Army, *Operational Law Handbook* (2002), quoted in Adam Roberts, 'The laws of war in the war on terror', in Fred L. Borch and Paul S. Wilson, eds, *International Law and the War on Terror* (Newport: US Naval War College, 2003). My discussion owes much to Roberts' reconstruction and interpretation of the US developments.

15 US Department of Defense, *Conduct of the Persian Gulf War: Final Report to Congress*, April 1992, p. 663. The report was prepared under the auspices of then Undersecretary of Defense for Policy Paul Wolfowitz and directed by his deputy, I. Lewis Libby. The report is available at:
http://www.ndu.edu/library/epubs/cpgw.pdf.

16 Rosa Brooks, 'War everywhere: Rights, national security law, and the law of armed conflict in the age of terror', *University of Pennsylvania Law Review*, vol. 153 (2004), p. 682.

17 Human Rights Watch, *Ghost Prisoner: Two Years in Secret CIA Detention* (February 2007).

18 Eric Umansky, 'Who are the prisoners at Gitmo?', *Columbia Journalism Review*, 5 (September/October 2006); Human Rights Watch, 'US: Guantánamo Kids at Risk', 24 April 2003, http://hrw.org/english/docs/2003/04/24/usint5782.htm (accessed 25 September 2007).

19 Alistair Horne, *A Savage War of Peace: Algeria 1954–1962* (New York: Viking Press, 1977), p. 111.

20 For other historical examples of the US use of Article 5 tribunals, see Jennifer K. Elsea, *Treatment of 'Battlefield Detainees' in the War on Terrorism*, US Congressional Research Service Report RL31367, 23 January 2007, http://www.fas.org/sgp/crs/terror/RL31367.pdf.

21 Draft memorandum for William J. Haynes, General Counsel, Department of Defense from John Yoo, Deputy Assistant Attorney General and Robert Delahunty, Special Counsel, Re: 'Application of treaties and laws to al Qaeda and Taliban detainees', 9 January 2002, p. 42, available at: http://lawofwar.org/Yoo_Delahunty_Memo.htm (accessed 9 September 2007). This draft provided the basis for subsequent legal advice to the president from the attorney general and other officials.

22 Memorandum for Alberto R. Gonzales, Counsel to the President, from Jay S. Bybee, Assistant Attorney General, Re: 'Standards of

conduct for interrogation under 18 U.S.C. § 2340–2340A', 1
August 2002, and Letter from John C. Yoo to Alberto R.
Gonzales, 1 August 2002, reprinted in Mark Danner, *Torture and
Truth: America, Abu Ghraib, and the War on Terror* (New York: New
York Review of Books, 2004), pp. 115–66; quotation at p. 149.
See also the discussion in Seymour M. Hersh, 'The gray zone:
How a secret Pentagon program came to Abu Ghraib', *The New
Yorker*, 24 May 2004, and id., *Chain of Command: The Road from
9/11 to Abu Ghraib* (New York: HarperCollins, 2004).

23 Jennifer K. Elsea, *Treatment of 'Battlefield Detainees' in the War on
Terrorism*, Congressional Research Service Report RL31367, 23
January 2007, available at:
http://www.fas.org/sgp/crs/terror/RL31367.pdf. Original
references, mostly to the US Constitution, have been removed.

24 James Risen and Eric Lichtblau, 'Concern over wider spying
under new law', *New York Times*, 19 August 2007.

25 Brooks, 'War everywhere' (above, n. 16), p. 729.

26 *The Geneva Convention Relative to the Treatment of Prisoners of War*
(12 August 1949), Article 4(2). See the discussion in Knut
Dörmann, 'The legal situation of "unlawful, unprivileged
combatants"', *International Review of the Red Cross*, vol. 85, no.
849 (March 2003).

27 Hans-Peter Gasser, 'Acts of terror, "terrorism" and international
humanitarian law', *International Review of the Red Cross*, vol. 84
(2002), quoted in K. A. Cavanaugh, 'Rewriting law: The case of
Israel and the occupied territories', in David Wippman and
Matthew Evangelista, eds, *New Wars, New Laws? Applying the Laws
of War in 21st Century Conflicts* (Ardsley, NY: Transnational
Publishers, 2005), ch. 9, at p. 253.

28 Michael Newton, 'Unlawful belligerency after September 11:
History revisited and law revised', in David Wippman and
Matthew Evangelista, eds, *New Wars, New Laws? Applying the Laws
of War in 21st Century Conflicts* (Ardsley, NY: Transnational
Publishers, 2005), ch. 4, at p. 106.

29 Memorandum to Alberto R. Gonzales and William J. Haynes II
from Jay S. Bybee, Re: 'Application of treaties and laws to al Qaeda
and Taliban detainees', 22 January 2002, available at:
http://www.gwu.edu/~nsarchiv/NSAEBB/NSAEBB127/02.01.22.
pdf; Memorandum for Alberto R. Gonzales, from Jay S. Bybee,
Re: 'Status of Taliban forces under Article 4 of the Third Geneva

Convention of 1949', 7 February 2002, reprinted in Danner, *Torture and Truth* (above, n. 22), pp. 96–104.

30 Michael Byers, *War Law: International Law and Armed Conflict* (London: Atlantic Books, 2005), p. 128. A good overview of the issue is provided by Kenneth Watkin, 'Humans in the cross-hairs: Targeting and assassination in contemporary armed conflict', in David Wippman and Matthew Evangelista, eds, *New Wars, New Laws? Applying the Laws of War in 21st Century Conflicts* (Ardsley, NY: Transnational Publishers, 2005), ch. 6. See also the discussion by Joseph Blocher, *The Guantanamo Three Step*, 117 Yale L. J. Pocket Part 1 (2007), http://thepocketpart.org/2007/07/04/ blocher.html.

31 David Cole, 'Why the court said No', *New York Review of Books*, vol. 53, no. 13 (10 August 2006).

32 The text of the decision, issued by Justice John Paul Stevens, is found at: http://www.law.cornell.edu/supct/html/05–184.ZO.html.

33 Rosa Brooks, 'Did Bush commit war crimes?' *Los Angeles Times*, 30 June 2006; Cole, 'Why the court said No' (above, n. 31).

34 Military Commissions Act of 2006, Public Law 109–366, 17 October 2006, available at: http://www.washingtonpost.com/wp-srv/politics/documents/cheney/military_commissions_act.pdf (accessed 24 September 2007).

35 Heather MacDonald, 'How to interrogate terrorists', *City Journal* (Winter 2005). All of the following quotations from MacDonald come from this article.

36 Mark Danner analyses the Schlesinger report and includes it as an appendix in *Torture and Truth* (above, n. 22).

37 In addition to the sources cited above, see Mark Bowden, 'The dark art of interrogation', *The Atlantic Monthly* (October 2003); Jane Mayer, 'A deadly interrogation: Can the C.I.A. legally kill a prisoner?' *The New Yorker*, 14 November 2005; Mayer, 'The black sites', *The New Yorker*, 13 August 2007; Alfred W. McCoy, *A Question of Torture: CIA Interrogation from the Cold War to the War on Terror* (New York: Metropolitan Books, 2006); Jennifer K. Harbury, *Truth, Torture, and the American Way: The History and Consequences of US Involvement in Torture* (Boston, MA: Beacon Press, 2005). Danner, *Torture and Truth* (above, n. 22), contains several of the key military investigative reports as appendices.

38 Jeffrey Rosen, 'Conscience of a conservative', *New York Times Magazine*, 9 September 2007, p. 46.
39 Action Memo from William J. Haynes II, General Counsel, to Secretary of Defense, 27 November 2002, reprinted in Danner, *Torture and Truth* (above, n. 22), pp. 181–2.
40 Susskind, *One Percent Doctrine* (above, n. 7), p. 152.
41 Charlie Savage, 'Bush could bypass new torture ban: Waiver right is reserved', *Boston Globe*, 4 January 2006; Jonathan S. Landay, 'Cheney calls "waterboarding" a valuable interrogation tool', *Miami Herald*, 26 October 2006.
42 Catherine Philp, 'CIA admits waterboarding of terror suspects', *The Times*, 7 February 2008, online version, http://www.timesonline.co.uk/tol/news/world/us_and_americas/article3321297.ece .
43 'History of an interrogation technique: Water Boarding', ABC News, 29 November 2005, http://abcnews.go.com/WNT/Investigation/story?id=1356870.
44 McCoy, *A Question of Torture* (above, n. 37); Harbury, *Truth, Torture, and the American Way* (above, n. 37); Mayer, 'Black sites' (above, n. 37).
45 Scott Shane, David Johnston, and James Risen, 'Secret US endorsement of severe interrogations', *New York Times*, 4 October 2007.
46 Tim Golden, 'Memo fueled deep rift in administration on detainees', *New York Times*, 1 October 2006; David Johnston, 'At a secret interrogation, dispute flared over tactics', *New York Times*, 10 September 2006; Bob Egelko, 'Psychologists' feud over aiding military interrogators coming to a head', *San Francisco Chronicle*, 18 August 2007; American Psychiatric Association, 'Psychiatric participation in interrogation of detainees', position statement, approved by the Board of Trustees and the Assembly of District Branches, May 2006, http://www.psych.org/edu/other_res/lib_archives/archives/ 200601.pdf.
47 Quoted in Danner, *Torture and Truth* (above, n. 22), p. 3.
48 Mayer, 'Black sites' (above, n. 37).
49 Shane, Johnston, and Risen, 'Secret US endorsement of severe interrogations' (above, n. 44).
50 Susskind, *One Percent Solution* (above, n. 7), pp. 99, 100, 115.
51 Scott Shane and Mark Mazzetti, 'Advisers fault harsh methods in interrogation', *New York Times*, 30 May 2007.

52 Ian Austen, 'Canadians fault U.S. for its role in torture case', *New York Times*, 19 September 2006.

53 First quotation from Reuters, 'German sues CIA in abduction case', 6 December 2005; second from Dana Priest, 'Wrongful imprisonment: Anatomy of a CIA mistake', *Washington Post*, 4 December 2005.

54 Tim Golden, 'In U.S. report, brutal details of 2 Afghan inmates; deaths', *New York Times*, 20 May 2005.

55 Tim Golden, 'Army faltered in investigating detainee abuse', *New York Times*, 22 May 2005.

56 Henry Shue, 'Response to Sanford Levinson', *Dissent* (Summer 2003).

57 Center for Constitutional Rights, Background brief on the case against Rumsfeld, Gonzales and others in Germany on November 14, 2006, http://www.ccr-ny.org/v2/GermanCase2006/extended summary.asp.

58 Thomas F. Hogan, Chief Judge, United States District Court for the District of Columbia, In Re: Iraq and Afghanistan Detainees Litigation, Memorandum Opinion, 27 March 2007.

59 Ward Thomas, *The Ethics of Destruction: Norms and Force in International Relations* (Ithaca, NY: Cornell University Press, 2001), p. 49.

60 Thomas, *Ethics of Destruction* (above), p. 83.

61 Testimony of Richard A. Clarke before the National Commission on Terrorist Attacks upon the United States, 24 March 2004, http://www.9-11commission.gov/hearings/hearing8/clarke_statement.pdf.

62 Michael Byers, *War Law: International Law and Armed Conflict* (London: Atlantic Books, 2005), pp. 57–8.

63 *The 9/11 Commission Report* (New York: W. W. Norton, n.d. (2004), pp. 97–8.

64 9/11 Commission Report, p. 98; Transcript of President Clinton's address, *New York Times*, 27 June 1993; Reuben E. Brigety II, *Ethics, Technology and the American Way of War: Cruise Missiles and US Security Policy* (London: Routledge, 2007), ch. 6.

65 William Safire, 'Slapping Saddam's wrist', *New York Times*, 28 June 1993.

66 Thomas, *Ethics of Destruction* (above, n. 59), pp. 49–50. A report on the CIA's most illegal activities, the so-called Family Jewels,

was declassified and released in June 2007, and is available at: http://www.gwu.edu/~nsarchiv/NSAEBB/NSAEBB222/index. htm.

67 Gary Solis, 'Targeted killing and the law of armed conflict', *Naval War College Review*, vol. 60, no. 3 (Spring 2007).

68 Quotations from Michael R. Gordon and Bernard E. Trainor, *Cobra II: The Inside Story of the Invasion and Occupation of Iraq* (New York: Pantheon Books, 2006), pp. 175, 169; see also Thomas E. Ricks, *Fiasco: The American Military Adventure in Iraq* (New York: Penguin Press, 2006), pp. 116–17.

69 'Off target: The conduct of the war and civilian casualties in Iraq', December 2003, http://www.hrw.org/reports/2003/usa1203/.

70 David Margolick, 'Israel's payback principle', *Vanity Fair* (January 2003).

71 See especially Roberts, 'The laws of war in the war on terror' (above, n. 14) and Brooks, 'War everywhere' (above, n. 16). For application to the Israeli–Palestinian conflict, see Cavanaugh, 'Rewriting law' (above, n. 27).

72 Cavanaugh, 'Rewriting law' (above, n. 27), pp. 250–3.

73 Watkin, 'Humans in the cross-hairs' (above, n. 30), pp. 156–7.

74 Margolick, 'Israel's payback principle' (above, n. 70).

75 Both quoted in Eben Kaplan, 'Targeted killings', Report 9627 of the Council on Foreign Relations, 2 March 2006, http://www.cfr.org/publication/9627/.

76 Paul von Zielbauer, 'Snipers baited and killed Iraqis, soldiers testify', *New York Times*, 25 September 2007.

77 David Rose, 'MI6 and CIA "sent student to Morocco to be tortured" ', *Observer* (London), 11 December 2005; Human Rights Watch, *Morocco: Counter-Terror Crackdown Sets Back Rights Progress*, 21 October 2004, http://hrw.org/english/docs/2004/10/21/morocc9522.htm.

CHAPTER 4 PREVENTIVE WAR: AN EMERGING NORM?

1 The texts are found at: http://daccessdds.un.org/doc/UNDOC/GEN/N01/533/82/PDF/N0153382.pdf?OpenElement and http://daccessdds.un.org/doc/UNDOC/GEN/N01/557/43/PDF/N0155743.pdf?OpenElement.

2 For a summary of their views, see Neta Crawford, 'Just war theory
  and the U.S. counterterror war', *Perspectives on Politics*, vol. 1, no. 1
  (March 2003).
3 Sheryl Gay Stolberg, 'Kennedy says war in Iraq was choice, not
  necessity', *New York Times*, 15 January 2004.
4 The National Security Strategy of the United States of America,
  September 2002, Washington, DC: The White House, available
  at: http://www.whitehouse.gov/nsc/nss.pdf. For an evaluation
  and critique, see Jonathan Kirshner, Barry Strauss, Maria Fanis,
  and Matthew Evangelista, 'Iraq and beyond: The new U.S.
  national security strategy', Occasional Paper #27, Peace Studies
  Program Cornell University, January 2003; Robert Jervis,
  'Understanding the Bush doctrine', *Political Science Quarterly*
  (November 2003); Neta C. Crawford, 'The false promise of
  collective security through preventive war: The "New Security
  Consensus" and a more insecure world', ch. 4 in Henry Shue and
  David Rodin, eds, *Preemption: Military Action and Moral
  Justification* (Oxford: Oxford University Press, 2007); Ugo Villani,
  'The war against Iraq, the United Nations, and international law',
  in Nicola Cufaro Petroni, ed., *Unilateral Actions and Military
  Interventions: The Future of Non-proliferation* (Bari, Italy: Servizio
  Editoriale Universitario, 2004), pp. 33–54.
5 Consider the advertisement that thirty-three scholars of the
  Realist School of International Relations put out in the *New York
  Times* on 25 September 2002 under the title, 'War with Iraq is *not*
  in America's national interest'. For a further discussion of their
  arguments, see the article by two of the signers, John J.
  Mearsheimer and Stephen M. Walt, ' "Realists" are not alone in
  opposing war with Iraq', *Chronicle of Higher Education*, 15
  November 2002.
6 Arthur F. Lykke, ed., *Military Strategy: Theory and Application*
  (Carlisle Barracks, PA: US Army War College, 1993), p. 386, cited
  in (Lieutenant Colonel) Michael J. Arinello, *National Security
  Strategy of Preemption*, US Army War College, Carlisle Barracks,
  PA, 18 March 2005, available at: http://www.strategic
  studiesinstitute.army.mil/pdffiles/ksil68.pdf.
7 Mearsheimer and Walt, ' "Realists" are not alone in opposing war
  with Iraq' (above, n. 5).
8 Joan Didion, 'Cheney: The fatal touch', *New York Review of Books*,
  vol. 53, no. 15 (5 October 2006).

9 Quoted in Ron Susskind, *The One Percent Doctrine: Deep Inside America's Pursuit of Its Enemies since 9/11* (New York: Simon and Schuster, 2006), p. 19.

10 Susskind, *One Percent Doctrine* (above), p. 23.

11 Didion, 'Cheney: The fatal touch' (above, n. 8).

12 Stephen Kull, *Misperceptions, the Media and the Iraq War* (College Park, MD: Program on International Policy Attitudes, 2003); Frank Rich, *The Greatest Story Ever Sold: The Decline and Fall of Truth from 9/11 to Katrina* (New York: Penguin, 2006); Zogby International, 'US troops in Iraq: 72% say end war in 2006', 28 February 2006, http://zogby.com/news/ReadNews. dbm?ID=1075; Chris Hedges and Laila Al-Arian, 'The other war', *The Nation*, 30 July/6 August 2007.

13 Susskind, *One Percent Doctrine* (above, n. 9), ch. 2.

14 Ibid., esp. pp. 50–1.

15 Ibid., pp. 61–2.

16 State of the Union address, 29 January 2002, http://www. whitehouse.gov/news/releases/2002/01/20020129–11.html.

17 'Bush and preventive war', *Air Force Magazine*, online edition, June 2007, vol. 90, no. 6, http://www.afa.org/magazine/June 2007/0607keeper.asp.

18 National Security Strategy of the United States, September 2002, p. 15.

19 James Mann, *Rise of the Vulcans: The History of Bush's War Cabinet* (New York: Viking, 2004), p. 327.

20 Graham T. Allison and Philip Zelikow, *Essence of Decision: Explaining the Cuban Missile Crisis*, 2nd edn (Reading, MA: Longman, 1999).

21 Stephen Kinzer, *Overthrow: America's Century of Regime Change from Hawaii to Iraq* (New York: Times Books, 2006).

22 Patrick Tyler, 'After the war, US juggling Iraq policy," *New York Times*, 13 April 1991.

23 Timothy Noah, 'Dick Cheney, Dove', *Slate*, 12 October 2002, http://www.slate.com/id/2072609/. Noah, whose article includes the other quotations as well, added the emphasis to the last one.

24 Michael R. Gordon and Bernard E. Trainor, *Cobra II: The Inside Story of the Invasion and Occupation of Iraq* (New York: Pantheon Books, 2006); Thomas E. Ricks, *Fiasco: The American Military Adventure in Iraq* (New York: Penguin Press, 2006).

25 The Pentagon study, summarized in Mann, *Rise of the Vulcans* (above, n. 19), pp. 81–2, is dated 15 June 1979 and was de-classified in April 2003. Ross is Mann's source for the Wolfowitz quotation.

26 Mann, *Rise of the Vulcans* (above, n. 19), p. 83.

27 For an overview of the relevant history and for access to the documents, see Joyce Battle, ed., *Shaking Hands with Saddam Hussein: The U.S. Tilts toward Iraq, 1980–1984*, National Security Archive Electronic Briefing Book No. 82, 25 February 2003, http://www.gwu.edu/~nsarchiv/NSAEBB/NSAEBB82/index.htm. The US was also complicit in chemical attacks against Iraqi Kurds. See Joost Hiltermann, *A Poisonous Affair: America, Iraq, and the Gassing of Halabja* (Cambridge, UK: Cambridge University Press, 2007) and Andrew Cockburn's review in *The Nation*, 7 September 2007.

28 Didion, 'Cheney: The fatal touch' (above, n. 8).

29 Coalition Provisional Authority, 'Iraq resolution endorses plan for transition, elections, June 8, 2004' (including text of UN Security Council Resolution 1546; emphasis in original), http://www.cpa-iraq.org/transcripts/20040609_UNSCR_Text.html. In November 2006 the Security Council, in Resolution 1723, extended the mandate until the end of 2007, http://www.un.org/News/Press/docs/2006/sc8879.doc.htm (both sites accessed 22 September 2007). For an important study of this issue, see Carlos Yordán, 'Why did the UN Security Council support the Anglo-American project to transform postwar Iraq? The evolution of international law in the shadow of the American hegemon', *Journal of International Law and International Relations*, vol. 3, no. 1 (Spring 2007).

30 Michael Byers, *Custom, Power and the Power of Rules: International Relations and Customary International Law* (Cambridge, UK: Cambridge University Press, 1999), pp. 163–4.

31 *Prosecutor v. Tadić* (Appeal on Jurisdiction, 2 October 1995), para. 99, quoted in Byers, *Custom, Power and the Power of Rules* (above), p. 163.

32 Peter Dombrowski and Rodger A. Payne, 'The emerging consensus for preventive war', *Survival*, vol. 48, no. 2 (2006), pp. 115–36, quotations at p. 120.

33 General Iurii Baluevskii, quoted in 'Russia to use Israel's methods to fight against terrorism', pravda.ru, 27 August 2005, from Johnson's Russia List, an e-mail newsletter.

34 For background, see http://www.globalsecurity.org/wmd/
    systems/rnep.htm.
35 Report of the High-Level Panel on Threats, Challenges and
    Change, *A More Secure World: Our Shared Responsibility* (New
    York: United Nations, 2004), para. 191.
36 Nicholas J. Wheeler, *Saving Strangers: Humanitarian Intervention
    in International Society* (Oxford, UK: Oxford University Press,
    2000), p. 293. This is an example of some of the excellent work
    by political scientists. Another is Richard Price, 'Emerging
    customary norms and anti-personnel landmines', in Christian
    Reus-Smit, *The Politics of International Law* (Cambridge, UK:
    Cambridge University Press, 2004), ch. 5.
37 Price, 'Emerging customary norms' (above), p. 114; see also
    Byers, *Custom, Power and the Power of Rule* (above, n. 30), esp.
    pp. 129–31.
38 Dombrowski and Payne, 'The emerging consensus for
    preventive war' (above, n. 32), p. 127, quoting Christina M.
    Schweiss, 'Sharing hegemony: The future of transatlantic
    security', *Cooperation and Conflict: Journal of the Nordic
    International Studies Association*, vol. 38, no. 3 (September 2003),
    pp. 211–34.
39 Crawford, 'The false promise of collective security' (above, n. 4).
40 Gilbert Burnham, Riyadh Lafta, Shannon Doucy, and Les
    Roberts, 'Mortality after the 2003 invasion of Iraq: A cross-
    sectional cluster sample survey', *The Lancet* (online), 11 October
    2006, http://web.mit.edu/CIS/lancet-study-101106.pdf; Rhoda
    Margesson, Jeremy M. Sharp, and Andorra Bruno, *Iraqi Refugees
    and Internally Displaced Persons: A Deepening Humanitarian
    Crisis?* US Congressional Research Service Report RL33936, 3
    October 2007.
41 The National Intelligence Estimate, *Trends in Global Terrorism:
    Implications for the United States* (April 2006), is still classified,
    but a summary of its main conclusions is available at http://www.
    globalsecurity.org/intell/library/reports/2006/nie_global-terror-
    trends_apr2006.htm (accessed 23 September 2006). On the
    various rationales for the war, see Chaim Kaufmann, 'Threat
    inflation and the failure of the marketplace of ideas: The selling of
    the Iraq War', *International Security*, vol. 29, no. 1 (Summer
    2004).

CHAPTER 5 HUMANITARIAN OBJECTIVES IN
ANTI-TERROR WARS

1 Kenneth Anderson, 'Humanitarian inviolability in crisis: The
   meaning of impartiality and neutrality for U.N. and NGO agencies
   following the 2003–2004 Afghanistan and Iraq conflicts', *Harvard
   Human Rights Journal*, vol. 17 (Spring 2004), p. 41.
2 Caroline Moorehead, *Dunant's Dream: War, Switzerland and the
   History of the Red Cross* (New York: Carroll and Graf, 1998), p. 298.
3 David P. Forsythe, 'The ICRC: A unique humanitarian
   protagonist', *International Review of the Red Cross*, vol. 89, no. 865
   (March 2007), p. 63. See also David P. Forsythe, *The
   Humanitarians: The International Committee of the Red Cross*
   (Cambridge, UK: Cambridge University Press, 2005).
4 Francis Fukuyama, 'The end of history?' *The National Interest*
   (Summer 1989); George H. W. Bush 'Toward a new world order',
   transcript of address to joint session of Congress, 11 September
   1990, available at: http://en.wikisource.org/wiki/
   Toward_a_New_World_Order.
5 Adam Roberts, 'The so-called "right" of humanitarian
   intervention', in *Yearbook of International Humanitarian Law 2000*,
   vol. 3 (The Hague: T.M.C. Asser, 2002), quoted in Thomas G.
   Weiss, *Humanitarian Intervention: Ideas in Action* (Cambridge,
   UK: Polity, 2007).
6 Independent International Commission on Kosovo, *Kosovo
   Report: Conflict, International Response, Lessons Learned* (Oxford,
   UK: Oxford University Press, 2000). For eyewitness accounts of
   the expulsions, see Tim Judah, *Kosovo: War and Revenge* (New
   Haven, CT: Yale University Press, 2000).
7 Tom Malinowski, interviewed by Julie A. Mertus, *Bait and Switch:
   Human Rights and US Foreign Policy* (New York: Routledge,
   2004), p. 151.
8 Nicolas de Torrenté, 'Humanitarian action under attack:
   Reflections on the Iraq War', *Harvard Human Rights Journal*, vol.
   17 (Spring 2004), p. 1.
9 De Torrenté, 'Humanitarian action' (above), p. 4; Mary Kaldor,
   New and Old Wars: Organized Violence in a Global Era, 2nd edn
   (Cambridge, UK: Polity, 2006).
10 Laura Silber and Allan Little, *Yugoslavia: Death of a Nation*, revised
   edn (New York: Penguin, 1997), p. 244.

11 Fiona Terry, *Condemned to Repeat? The Paradox of Humanitarian Action* (Ithaca, NY: Cornell University Press, 2002).

12 Ewen MacAskill, 'Britain fought to block UN sanctions against Taliban', *Guardian*, 22 December 2000; Mary Ellen O'Connell, 'Enhancing the status of non-state actors through a global war on terror', *Columbia Journal of Transnational Law*, vol. 43, no. 2 (2004), pp. 443–4.

13 Radio Address by Mrs. Bush, Crawford, Texas, Office of the First Lady, the White House, 17 November 2001, http://www.whitehouse.gov/news/releases/2001/11/20011117.html.

14 De Torrenté, 'Humanitarian action' (above, n. 8), p. 3.

15 Phillip James Walker, 'Iraq and occupation', in David Wippman and Matthew Evangelista, eds, *New Wars, New Laws? Applying the Laws of War in 21st Century Conflicts* (Ardsley, NY: Transnational Publishers, 2005), ch. 10, quotations at pp. 265–6.

16 Walker, 'Iraq and occupation' (above), includes some examples, but see especially the first-hand, on-the-record accounts in Chris Hedges and Laila Al-Arian, 'The other war', *The Nation*, 30 July/6 August 2007.

17 Secretary Colin L. Powell, 'Remarks to the National Foreign Policy Conference for Leaders of Nongovernmental Organizations', US Department of State, Washington, DC, 26 October 2001; De Torrenté, 'Humanitarian action' (above, n. 8), pp. 8–10; Luca Rastello, 'L'imperativo umanitario e le sue ambiguità', *Biblioteca della Libertà*, vol. 40, n. 178 (January/March 2005).

18 Andrew Natsios's remarks at a May 2003 Fo(above, n. 7), p. 188, and available at: http://www.interaction.org/forum2003/panels.html.

19 De Torrenté, 'Humanitarian action' (above, n. 8), p. 12.

20 Bronwyn Leebaw, 'The politics of impartial activism: Humanitarianism and human rights', *Perspectives on Politics*, vol. 5, no. 2 (June 2007).

21 Mertus, *Bait and Switch* (above, n. 7), p. 151.

22 Gary J. Bass, 'Jus post bellum', *Philosophy and Public Affairs*, vol. 32, no. 4 (September 2004); Louis V. Iasiello, 'Jus post bellum: The moral responsibilities of victors in war', *Naval War College Review*, vol. 57 (2004).

23 Richard W. Stevenson, 'Bush says patience is needed as nations build a democracy', *New York Times*, 19 May 2005.

24 Peter W. Singer, *Corporate Warriors: The Rise of the Privatized Military Industry* (Ithaca, NY: Cornell University Press, 2003); Carolina Sassi, 'Le compagnie militari private. Guida all'approfondimento', *Biblioteca della Libertà*, vol. 40, n. 178 (January/March 2005).

25 Weiss, *Humanitarian Intervention* (above, n. 5), pp. 76, 74.

26 Anderson, 'Humanitarian inviolability' (above, n. 1), p. 74.

27 Celia W. Dugger, 'CARE turns down federal funds for food aid', *New York Times*, 16 August 2007.

28 On links between mercenaries past and present, see Fabio Armao, 'La rinascita del privateering: Lo Stato e il nuovo mercato della guerra', in Angelo d'Orsi, ed., *Guerre globali: Capire i conflitti del XXI secolo* (Rome: Carocci editore, 2003); James Cockayne, 'The global reorganization of legitimate violence: Military entrepreneurs and the private face of international humanitarian law', *International Review of the Red Cross*, vol. 88, no. 863 (September 2006).

29 Philippe Le Billon, ed., *The Geopolitics of Resource Wars*, special issue of *Geopolitics*, vol. 9, no. 1 (Summer 2004); Deborah D. Avant, *The Market for Force: The Consequences of Privatizing Security* (Cambridge, UK: Cambridge University Press, 2005); id., 'The marketization of security: Adventurous defense, institutional malformation, and conflict', in Jonathan Kirshner, ed., *Globalization and National Security* (London: Routledge, 2006), ch. 4; Jeremy Scahill, *Blackwater: The Rise of the World's Most Powerful Mercenary Army* (New York: Nation Books, 2007).

30 Weiss, *Humanitarian Intervention* (above, n. 5), p. 138.

31 Associated Press, 'Gates sending investigators to Iraq', 26 September 2007. The Pentagon's figure for 'private security contractors working for the Pentagon in Iraq', reported in this article, is 7,300, but it presumably does not include armed contractors not working directly in security.

32 Joan Didion, 'Cheney: The fatal touch', *New York Review of Books*, vol. 53, no. 15 (5 October 2006).

33 Geoffrey Best, *Humanity in Warfare* (New York: Columbia University Press, 1980), pp. 374–5, n. 83.

34 P. W. Singer, 'War, profits, and the vacuum of law: Privatized military firms and international law', *Columbia Journal of Transnational Law*, vol. 42, no. 2 (2004), p. 531, original emphasis.

35 Hedges and Al-Arian, 'The other war' (above, n. 16).

36 I am grateful to an anonymous reviewer for the clarification of some of the issues addressed in this paragraph and the next. For a summary of the latest legislation, see Human Rights Watch, 'Q&A: Private military contractors and the law', http://hrw.org/english/docs/2004/05/05/iraq8547_txt.htm (accessed 23 November 2007).

37 Scahill, *Blackwater*; on the September 2007 incident, see James Rise, 'State Dept. tallies 56 shootings involving Blackwater on diplomatic guard duty', *New York Times*, 28 September 2007; James Glanz and Sabrina Tavernise, 'Scene of Blackwater shooting was chaotic', *New York Times*, 28 September 2007; John M. Border and James Risen, 'Blackwater tops all firms in Iraq in shooting rate', *New York Times*, 27 September 2007.

38 Human Rights Watch, 'Q&A: Private military contractors and the law' (above, n. 36).

39 Gates is quoted in Associated Press, 'Iraq drafts law on security companies', 26 September 2007.

40 Cockayne, 'Global reorganization of legitimate violence' (above, n. 28), p. 477.

41 Editorial, *International Review of the Red Cross*, no. 863 (September 2006), a special issue on private military companies, pp. 445–8, available at: http://www.icrc.org/Web/Eng/ siteengo.nsf/html/review-863-p445.

42 Border and Risen, 'Blackwater tops all firms' (above, n. 37).

43 Leslie Wayne, 'America's for-profit secret army', *New York Times*, 13 October 2002.

44 Ibid; Sarah Mendelson, *Barracks and Brothels: Peacekeeping and Human Trafficking in the Balkans* (Washington, DC: Center for International and Strategic Studies, 2005); Avant, *Market for Force* (above, n. 29).

45 David Wippman and Henry Shue, 'Limiting attacks on dual-use facilities performing indispensable civilian functions', *Cornell International Law Journal*, vol. 35 (2002), pp. 559–79; see also Thomas W. Smith, 'The new law of war: Legitimizing hi-tech and infrastructure violence', *International Studies Quarterly*, vol. 46, no. 3 (September 2002).

46 Human Rights Watch, 'Needless deaths in the Gulf War: Civilian casualties during the air campaign and violations of the laws of war', 1991, http://www.hrw.org/reports/1991/gulfwar/;

'Civilian deaths in the NATO air campaign [Kosovo]', February 2000, http://www.hrw.org/reports/2000/nato/index. htm#TopOfPage; 'Fatally flawed: cluster bombs and their use by the United States in Afghanistan', December 2002, http://hrw.org/reports/2002/us-afghanistan/; 'Off target: The conduct of the war and civilian casualties in Iraq', December 2003, http://www.hrw.org/reports/2003/usa1203/; 'Backgrounder on Russian fuel air explosives ("vacuum bombs")', February 2000, http://www.hrw.org/press/ 2000/02/checho215b.htm; 'War crimes in Chechnya and the response of the West', Testimony before the US Senate Committee on Foreign Relations by Peter Bouckaert, Human Rights Watch Emergencies Researcher, 1 March 2000, http://www.hrw.org/campaigns/russia/chechnya/peter-testimony.htm.

47 Human Rights Watch, 'Fatally flawed' (above) and 'Off target' (above).

48 Margarita Petrova, 'Curbing the use of indiscriminate weapons: NGO advocacy in militant democracies', in Matthew Evangelista, Harald Müller, and Niklas Schörnig, eds, *Democracy and Security: Preferences, Norms, and Policy* (London: Routledge, 2008); id., *Leadership Competition and the Creation of Norms: A Crossnational Study of Weapons Restrictions* (PhD dissertation, Cornell University, Department of Government, January 2007).

49 Human Rights Watch, 'Chechen fighters endanger civilian lives: "Shielding" violates laws of war', 13 January 2000, http://www.hrw.org/press/2000/01/checho114.htm; 'Human shields in Iraq put obligations on U.S.', 20 February 2003, http://hrw.org/press/2003/02/iraq0220.htm; 'Iraqi landmines found in Mosque, condemned as violation of international law', 2 April 2003, http://www.hrw.org/press/2003/04/iraqo 40203.htm.

50 Stephen Watts, 'Air war and restraint: The role of public opinion and democracy', in Evangelista, Müller, and Schörnig, eds, *Democracy and Security* (above, n. 48). For the argument that authoritarian regimes also face 'audience costs', see Jessica Weeks, 'Autocratic audience costs: Regime type and signaling resolve', *International Organization*, vol. 62, no. 1 (Winter 2008).

CONCLUSION

1 David Rose, 'MI6 and CIA "sent student to Morocco to be
   tortured" ', *Observer* (London), 11 December 2005; Human Rights
   Watch, *Morocco: Counter-Terror Crackdown Sets Back Rights
   Progress*, 21 October 2004, http://hrw.org/english
   /docs/2004/10/21/morocc9522.htm.
2 Report of the Secretary General's High-Level Panel on Threats,
   Challenges and Change, *A More Secure World: Our Shared
   Responsibility* (New York: United Nations, 2004).
3 Kim Lane Scheppele, 'The migration of anti-constitutional ideas:
   The post-9/11 globalization of public law and the international
   state of emergency', in Sujit Choudhry, ed., *The Migration of
   Constitutional Ideas* (Cambridge, UK: Cambridge University
   Press, 2007), ch. 13.
4 Mary Robinson, UN High Commissioner for Human Rights,
   March 2002, http://www.unhchr.ch/huricane/huricane.nsf/
   view01/858EF20492884DD6C1256B82003E2A38?opendocument.
5 Craig Whitlock, 'In letter, radical cleric details CIA abduction,
   Egyptian torture', *Washington Post*, 10 November 2006;
   Associated Press, 'Italy indicts 31 in '03 C.I.A. abduction case', 16
   February 2007.
6 The Statewatch organization, based in Britain, reports on relevant
   developments in the Council on Europe and elsewhere at
   http://www.statewatch.org/cia/cia2.htm.
7 Neil A. Lewis, 'Military lawyers prepare to speak on Guantánamo',
   New York Times, 11 July 2006.
8 Catherine Powell, 'The role of transnational norm entrepreneurs
   in the US "war on terrorism" ', *Theoretical Inquiries in Law*, vol. 5
   (January 2004), pp. 48–80.
9 Kenneth Anderson, 'First in the field', *Times Literary Supplement
   Book Review*, 31 July 1998, available at: http://www.wcl.american.
   edu/faculty/anderson/first_in_the_field.pdf.

Index